ANGRAVE'S
AMAZING AUTOS

BRUCE ANGRAVE

Published by Frederick Warne (Publishers) Ltd, London, 1980

© text and illustrations Bruce Angrave, 1980

ISBN 0 7232 2711 X

Printed in Great Britain
by Butler & Tanner Ltd
Frome and London

ANGRAVE'S
AMAZING AUTOS

BRUCE ANGRAVE

FREDERICK WARNE

London

The Clustabus

The Clustabus looks rather like a fairground bumper car—more streamlined, of course, and equipped with windscreen, pneumatic tyres and its own small engine. The device distinguishing the Clustabus most significantly from a bumper car, however, is a system of couplings, one at the front (B), and the other behind (A).

Each Clustabus is just large enough to accommodate two people—or a parent and two children—in comfort and is designed particularly for the commuter, carrying him to and from his office with minimum stress. Parking, naturally, is easy and the fuel used is a fraction of that consumed by the old-fashioned jumbo car.

The commuter's wife has her own Clustabus for visiting friends, going shopping or collecting the children from school while he is away at work. Suppose, however, that the commuter wants to go for a run with his wife and two children on a Sunday afternoon. Simple: she couples her Clustabus behind her husband's. As the two vehicles come together the front coupling (B) of her Clustabus slides up the ramp-coupling (A) on the back of his. This lifts her front wheels off the road, converting the rear Clustabus into a two-wheeled trailer. A pin (C) automatically links the couplings together, while the accelerator, brake and other controls are hooked up by a cord (E), connected by plug (F) to socket (D). The two Clustabuses are now, in effect, a four-seater articulated vehicle. (When not in use the plug F is 'parked' in socket G).

If friends and relatives wish to join the commuter and his wife on their Sunday drive, they simply clip their Clustabuses on behind. Control of all the vehicles is automatically transferred to the leading Clustabus via the couplings and the composite vehicle still takes up little more room than that occupied by the commuter's old-fashioned jumbo car.

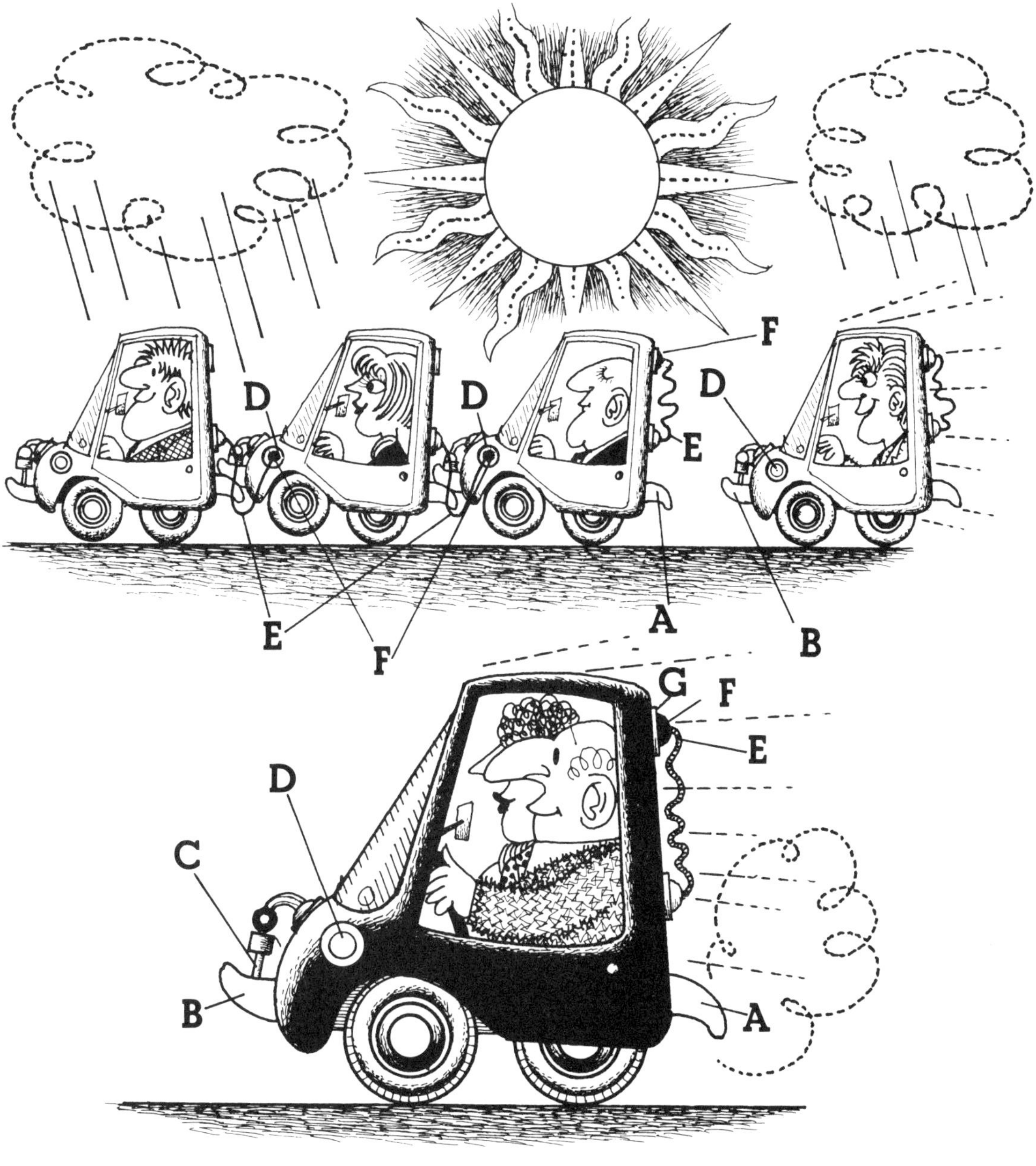
D
D
F
D
E
E
F
A
B
G
F
E
D
C
B
A

The Accordicar

This car can be folded, enabling it to be parked in the minimum of space. The bumpers serve a triple purpose, acting 1) as normal bumpers; 2) as stiffeners, to prevent the vehicle from folding up on itself and the driver when in motion; and 3) as levers, enabling the car to be accordionized with minimum effort.

The act of lifting one end of the bumper (X) causes it to pivot about a shaft (Y) at the other end. This operates a concealed linkage which pulls the offside (Z) of the car towards the kerb. At the same time, small 'jack-wheels' (V) set at right-angles to the roadwheels, are thrust down, lifting the side of the car slightly and enabling the offside tyres to slide easily over the road surface.

The problem of designing an effective wiper for an eight-panelled windscreen has not yet been satisfactorily resolved but the finest brains are working on it.

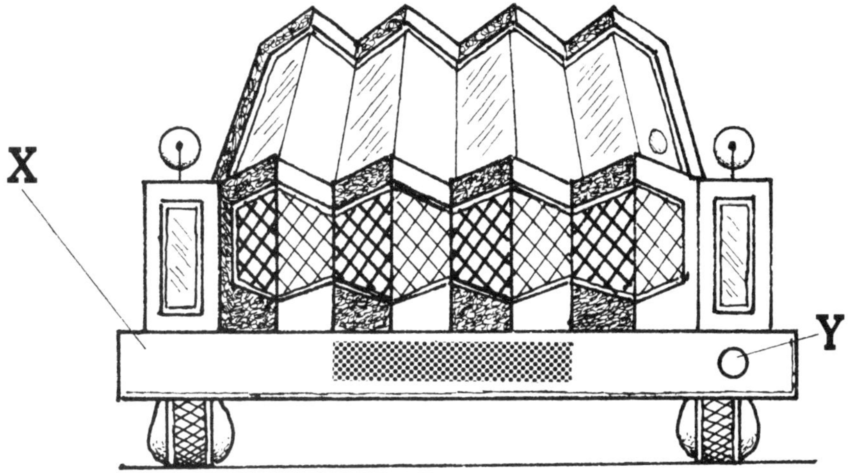
X
Y

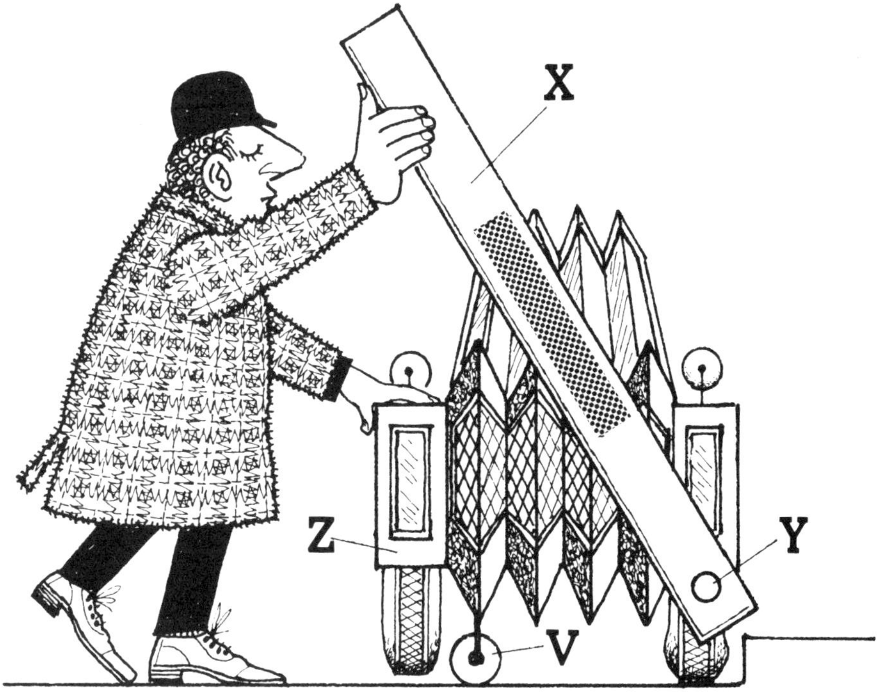
X
Z
Y
V

The Perisnork

What driver amongst us has not become uneasily aware, as he fumes in today's congested traffic, that fumes even more lethal than his own are stealing in through the nooks, crannies and ventilators of his car? Whereas his own fuming increases his blood pressure, speeds up his heart rate and tautens his nerves, the others, heavy as they are with carbon monoxide, lead-laden petrol by-products, particles of tar and the smell of burning rubber, affect his breathing and are injurious to his general health and vitality. The Perisnork eliminates at least the second source of fuming and by doing so undoubtedly lessens the first.

As so often with great inventions the basic principle is remarkably simple. Protruding through the front part of the car's roof is a tube (P). The lower end of this tube curves backwards (Q) towards the driver on a level with the eye-nose region, whilst the top end curves forwards (R). Fresh air from the vicinity of R is wafted down to the driver's nose at Q, bringing the health-giving benefits of an increased oxygen supply to his hard-pressed lungs. The Perisnork is retractable, so that the car can be housed in a garage of normal height, and is also extendable, ensuring that the freshest available air is always accessible. This adjustment of height is effected by a handcrank (S) which winds in a cord (T), retracting the Perisnork (normally kept fully extended by compression spring U).

Fitted into the bends of the Perisnork at V and W are mirrors arranged at angles of 45 degrees. The vehicle is thus provided with a periscope through which the driver can peer if he wants to see into or over the top of the bus in front. To aid this activity a lever (X) can be used to swivel the Perisnork from side to side. An additional refinement consists of a microphone (Y) connected through a small amplifier to a loudspeaker (Z). This collects the sounds of nature—birds singing, the rustle of leaves, and the soughing of the wind—usually drowned by the thunder of engines below.

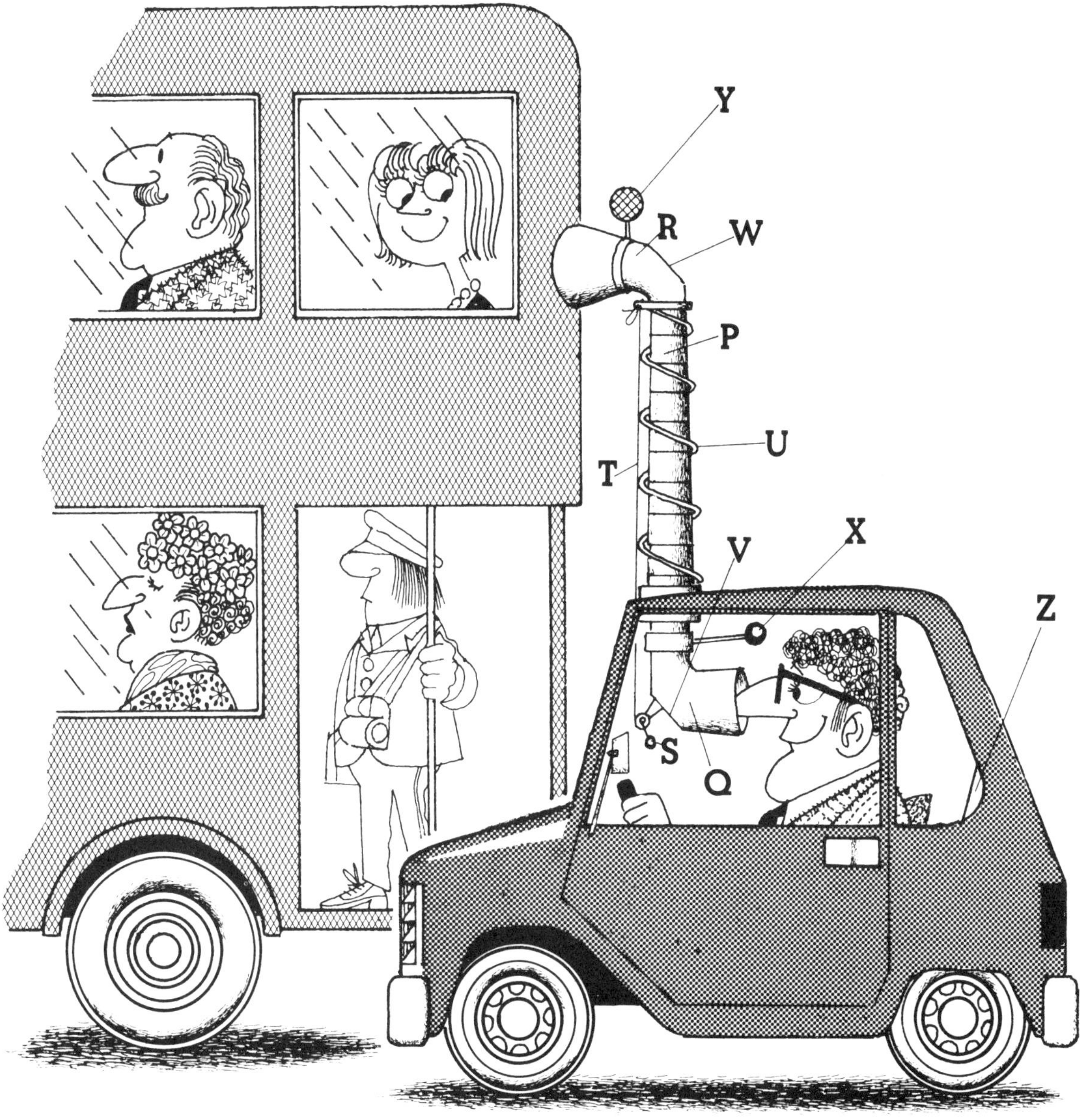
Y
R
W
P
U
T
X
V
Z
S
Q

The Overcar

The Overcar is designed in the form of a hump-backed bridge, with hinged ramps on trailing wheels mounted fore and aft. Thus it is incapable of collision. More conventional vehicles simply ride over it, as over a bump in the road. Other Overcars may ride over or under, the choice being controlled by an automatic device governed by the size of the trailing wheels. Little wheels are fitted as standard on cars of the limousine class, where dignity and poise are at a premium. By causing the leading edges of the ramps (A) to ride closer to the road surface, little wheels (B) ensure that the vehicle upon which they are installed shall ride *under* other vehicles and thus travel more smoothly and with less jolting. Larger wheels (C and D), on the other hand, make the dullest road a merry switchback and are greatly appreciated by all for whom violent physical motion is essential for the full enjoyment of life.

To avoid damage by overpassing car tyres, the wipers of the Overcar retract into recesses just below the windscreen. This happens automatically when weight is applied to the front ramp. Should two similarly-wheeled Overcars meet head-on, the risk of an old-fashioned collision is minimized because the trailing wheels are mounted eccentrically on their axles. This imparts a slight vertical wiggle to the ramps, ensuring that the leading edges of any two cars are never likely to be at exactly the same distance from the ground simultaneously. An exhilarating element of chance is introduced by this precaution as neither driver is able to tell in advance whether he is going over or under the approaching Overcar. The sporting motorist, incidentally, can drive over two Overcars at once (as at E) and literally 'take off'. To facilitate a reasonably safe landing, the front ramps (F) of the sports models are limited in their vertical movement and cannot drop down below the road wheels as at (G) on standard Overcars.

The introduction of the Overcar not only eliminates the hazard of head-on collisions. Much more than that, their universal use will double the country's effective road area. Every road would be converted into a two-directional one-way street, traffic in either direction using the full width of the road and simply riding over or under vehicles travelling the other way.

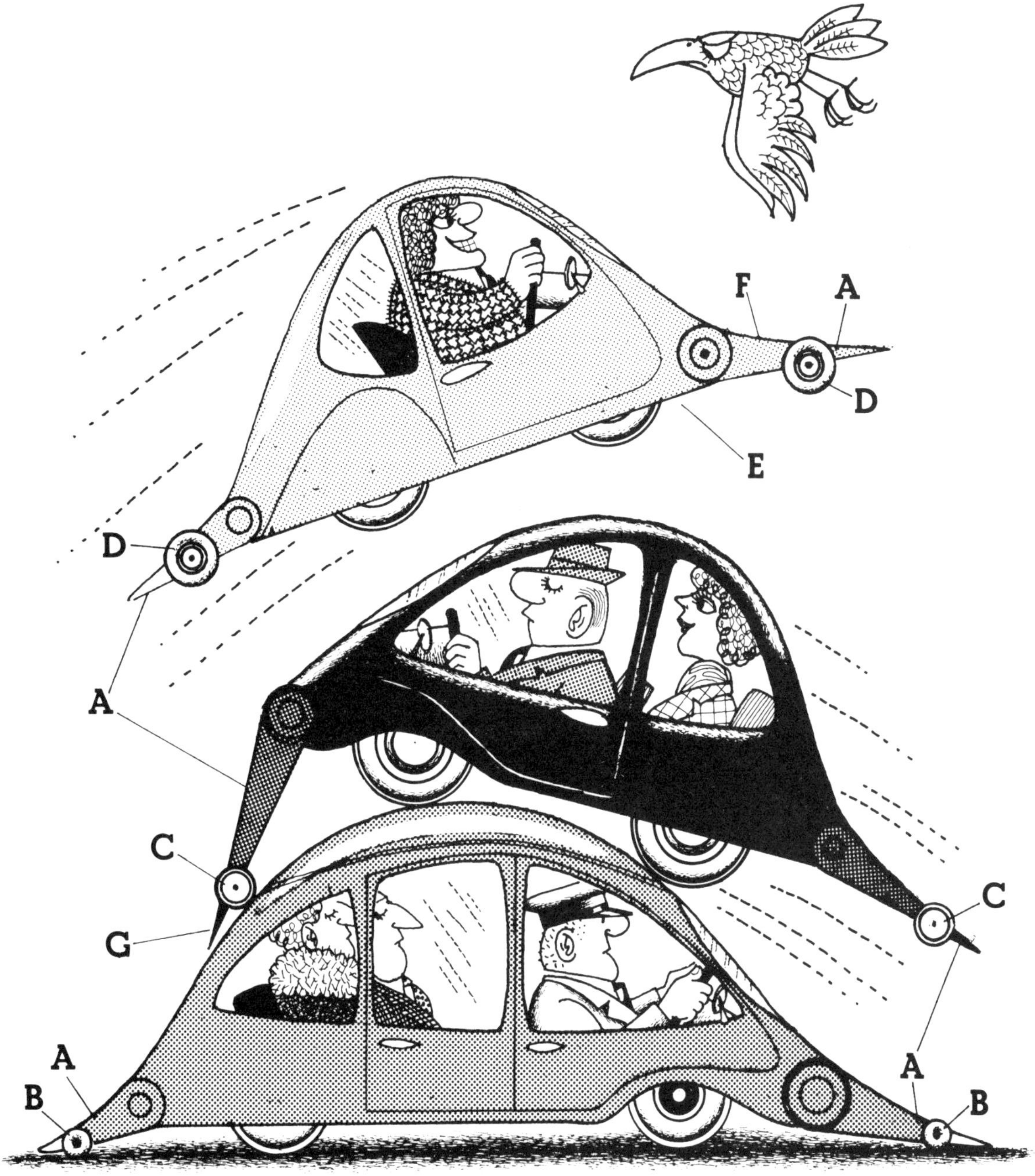
F
A
D
E
D
A
C
C
G
A
B
A
B

The Verticar

This vertical passenger-stacking vehicle, in its basic form a family car, is arranged with one seat above the other, each passenger sitting in his own little cabin (A), with windscreen, door and telephone (B) under his personal control. The telephone is for communication between driver (D) and passengers, absence of direct conversation being one of the many incidental advantages in this type of construction. Aided by the telephone, mother-in-law (C) can become a top, bottom or middle-seat driver to her heart's content, shouting directions and criticisms into the driver's ear as often as she likes. And, of course, there is nothing to prevent the driver taking his phone off the hook (E).

Instruments, pedals, gear and brake facilities are fitted on each level, so the driver can sit anywhere he likes in the Verticar, merely clipping his steering wheel (F) to the common steering column (G) which runs up through all the cabins. Thus if he likes a nice airy view of the countryside, or enjoys peering into apartment windows, he can take the top cabin, while if he prefers to study the infinite variety of human character on the pavements below, he can select the bottom one.

Access to the cabins of the Verticar is by ladder (H), though in Rolls-Royce, Mercedes and Cadillac Verticars an elevator can be installed for effortless ascent and descent. For increased stability on bad roads a helicopter rotor (J) can be provided at the top which, rotating at half-power, should give sufficient lift to keep the vehicle upright even on steep hills. When a low bridge is encountered, throttling down the rotor will enable the Verticar to lean over, pass under the obstruction and raise itself again.

The Verticar could come in various styles: a Classical Verticar would be shaped like a Greek column, with headlights in the volutes of the capital; or it could look like an upended intercontinental ballistic missile for giving suitably alarming impressions to the operators of spy satellites; or be built in the form of a factory chimney covered with advertisements, each yielding an acceptable sum in rent. The possibilities are limitless.

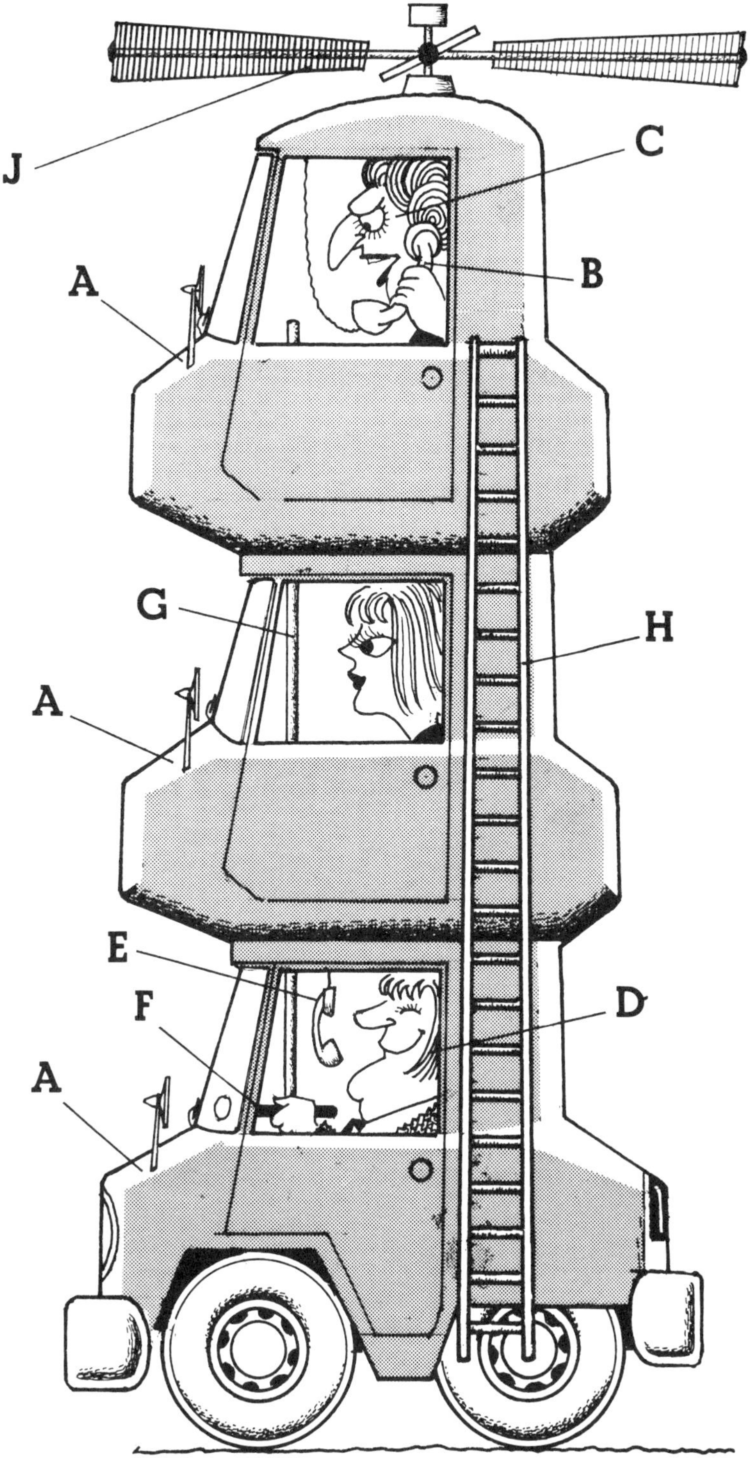
J
C
A
B
G
H
A
E
F
D
A

The Hovabile

The Hovabile can be parked off the ground. Its secret is a retractable hot-air balloon, normally concealed in the roof. When the driver wishes to park he releases the balloon (A) and diverts hot gases from the exhaust by a valve (B) to a vertical pipe under the balloon orifice (C). As the engine ticks over the balloon fills with lighter-than-air hot gas and the car rises from the road. (It is advisable to tether the vehicle to a nearby lamp-post (D) by means of a cord (E).) While the car is 'hovering' it is of course immune from the charge of 'Leaving a Stationary Vehicle with its Engine Running'. However, if the fuel should happen to give out the car will slowly descend to street level, the excuse 'Broken Down—Out of Petrol' inscribed on a card previously placed behind the windscreen ensuring no prosecution for illegal parking or obstruction.

When the driver returns to his vehicle and wishes to retrieve it he simply produces a rope (F) carried in his briefcase and lassoes the exhaust transfer valve lever, pulling it to its 'normal' position. This allows the car to descend.

At some extra cost a propeller (G), fixed to the front of the vehicle and connected to the engine drive-shaft, converts the car into a small dirigible or airship. A rudder (H) is added at the back, linked to the steering gear by cables (J). This modification is available only to those with a pilot's licence.

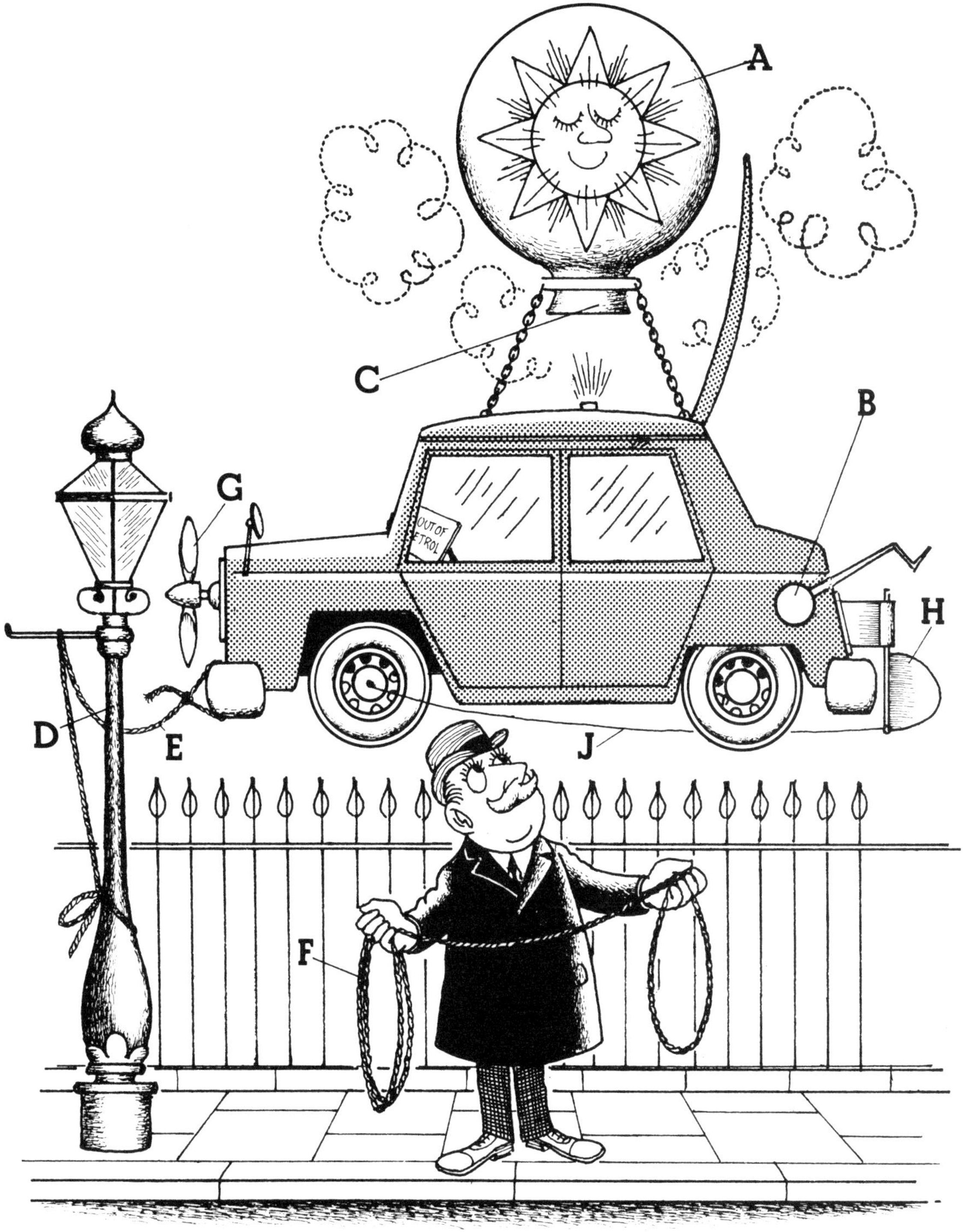
A
B
C
D
E
F
G
H
J
OUT OF
ETROL

The Wind Warden

The Wind Warden is a plastic inflatable traffic warden (T) which, in its deflated form, takes up next to no room in your glove compartment. The procedure is as follows: Park your car in any street, however busy, but preferably not on a double yellow line. Unroll the Wind Warden and connect a bicycle pump to the small valve (V) on the top of her cap. Inflate. The Wind Warden will assume an erect posture, holding a parking ticket (W) in one hand and a pencil (X) in the other. Now place her on the pavement beside your car (Y). You are then free to leave the vehicle for any reasonable length of time. Other traffic wardens will think your warden is booking you and take no action. On your return simply unscrew the valve (V) and deflate the Wind Warden, choosing a moment when a noisy vehicle is passing because the valve tends to whistle as she deflates. Roll up the deflated Wind Warden and place her back in your glove compartment.

The Wind Warden comes with a dual-purpose tube (Z) which connects her to the front nearside tyre of your car. This not only prevents her from floating away down the street, but also helps to keep her fully inflated in case of a leak. Should, notwithstanding all such precautions, a severe perforation cause her to subside in a crumpled plastic heap, the tyre will deflate too. This should be enough to avoid the consequences of a parking ticket, on the plea of breakdown.

N.B. It is advisable to make quite sure that the Wind Warden is indeed yours before you deflate her. It has been known for Wind Wardens to collapse after, for example, cats have sharpened their claws on them. Should this happen your Wind Warden could be replaced by a real one, resulting in charges of assault and battery as well as a parking ticket.

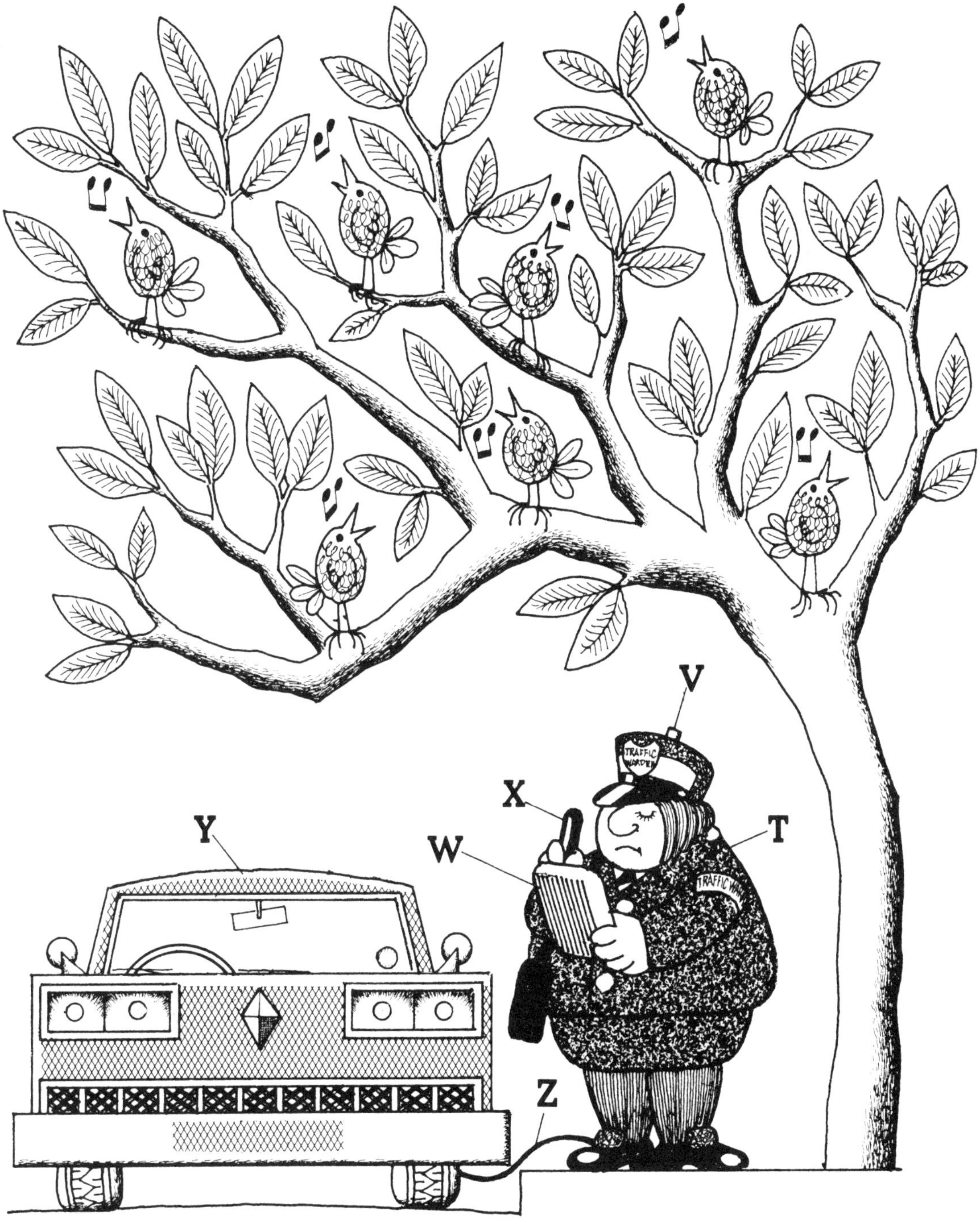
V
X
Y
W
T
Z
TRAFFIC

The Prioritomaton

Use of the Prioritomaton enables drivers to enter a busy main road from a side street without risk of collision. Suitable for most rear- or mid-engined cars, the Prioritomaton comprises a plastic housewife (A), dummy perambulator (B) and simulated baby (C), all mounted upside-down under the front-hinged bonnet (D).

The vehicle is driven to the main-road junction at the end of the side street and stopped as close as possible to the passing traffic. The bonnet, complete with plastic housewife, dummy perambulator and simulated baby, is then opened, either by hand-cranked linkage or, preferably, by button-operated electric motor controlled from the driver's seat. The hinged bonnet swings completely over so that its upper side rides close to the road surface (E), upside-down in front of the car. The plastic housewife, dummy perambulator and simulated baby are now right-way-up and also in front of the car. The vehicle then proceeds slowly but firmly into the main road, all traffic instantly stopping to allow the supposed housewife, perambulator and baby right of way on the principle, well established by legions of housewives on and off pedestrian crossings, that if you want to cross a road there is nothing like a baby in a perambulator, boldly propelled in front of you, for doing the trick. After the busy road has been entered the plastic housewife, dummy perambulator and simulated baby are folded back into the front of the car by means of a second button operated from the driver's seat.

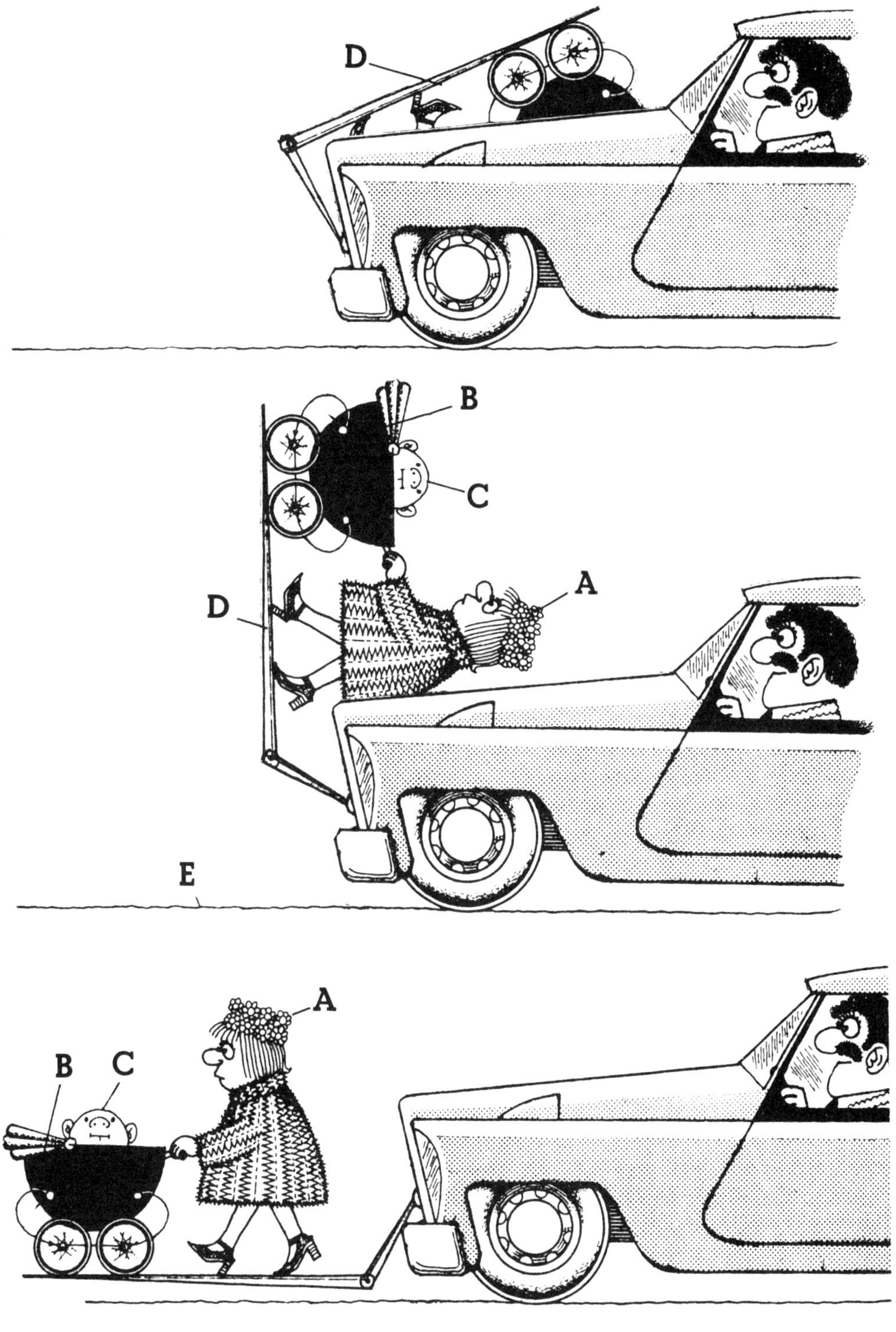
D
B
C
A
D
E
A
B
C

The Portacross

The Portacross can be carried easily by the average pedestrian and attracts little attention, looking as it does like a roll of linoleum. The 'linoleum' (A) is laid in the gutter and, at a suitable moment, is flicked across the road (B), unrolling rapidly and revealing itself as a striped pedestrian crossing (C). Four small lead weights (D) are already clipped to the Portacross, two at the outer edges of each end. The purpose of these is to hold the device down so that it does not roll itself up again. As the Portacross rolls across the road two orange balloons (E), filled with natural gas and tethered by black-and-white striped cord, float up, assuming the aspect of normal crossing beacons. The operator then steps on to the apparatus, causing all traffic to come grinding to a halt. He unclips the weights attached to the end nearest to him and traverses the road. As he crosses, the Portacross, relieved of its weights, rolls up behind him by reason of its natural springiness. Once on the opposite pavement, the rolled-up Portacross is gathered up and the pedestrian continues on his way not forgetting to re-attach the weights to what is now the inner edge of the Portacross, so that is is ready for further use.

If the pedestrian should become housebound the Portacross can be used as a floor covering and the balloons as party decorations at Christmas time.

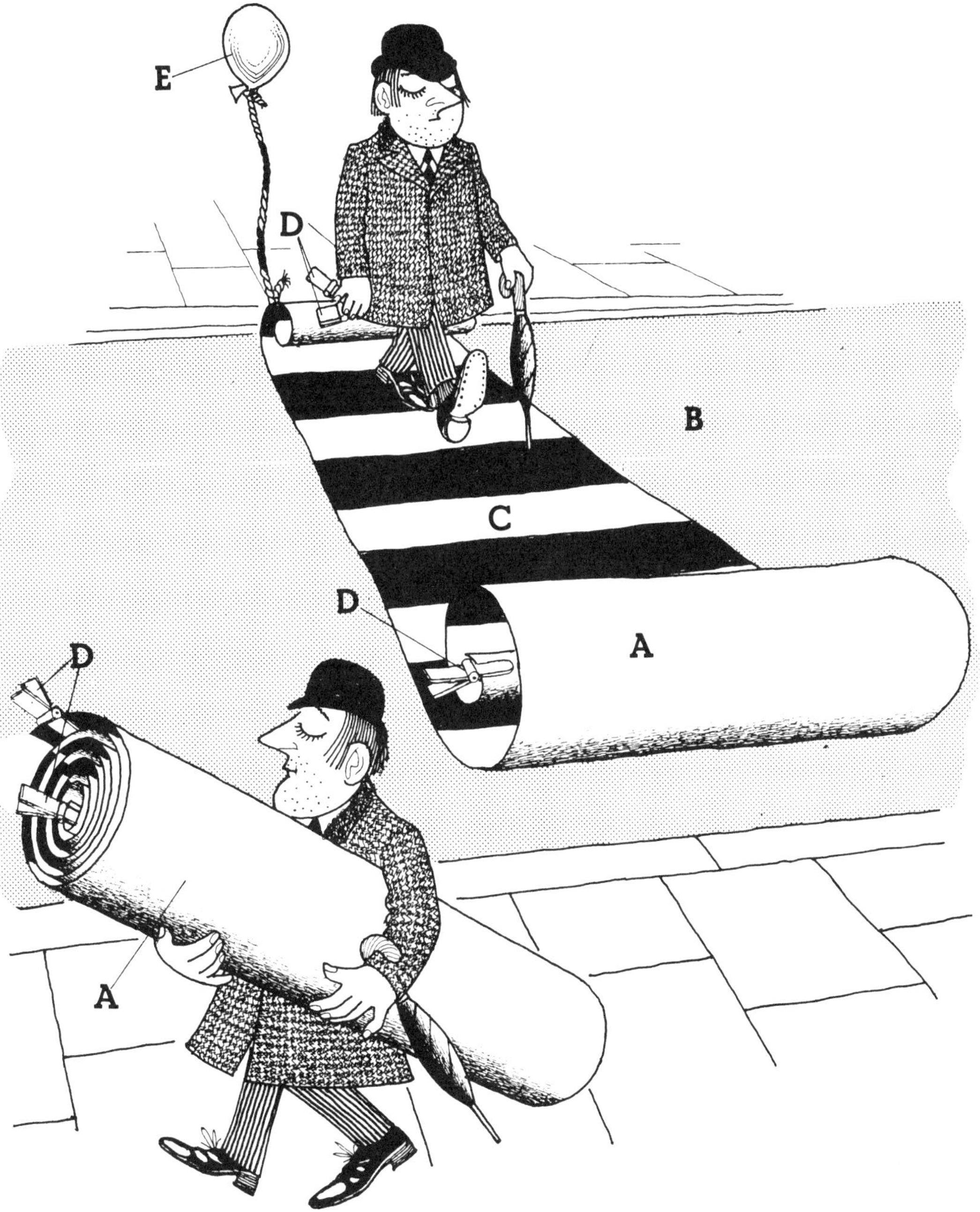
E
D
B
C
D
A
D
A

The Psychogrille

Motorists suffering from nervous frustration in traffic have few methods open to them for venting their displeasure. They can sound their horns, bellow lustily out of their windows, or cut in and gesticulate nastily. All these activities are dangerous, demeaning and liable to increase frustration instead of relieving it.

The Psychogrille is a flexible plastic radiator grille, connected by linkage and servo-motors to two sensing devices, a thermometer in the seat belt and a photoelectric eye aimed at the driver's face. As the driver's temperature rises, through rage and frustration, so the servo-motors pull the corners of the grille downwards into a scowl (A). Pressure on the horn button operates an overriding device which deepens the scowl into an expression of great hostility (C). The driver who keeps his cool does not activate these devices and the grille wears its normal expression (B). Should the driver's face turn purple with anger, the photoelectric eye operates the associated servos which respond with an expressive snarl up front, while a sudden ashen hue produces a grille full of fear, with starting headlamps.

It will be found that this device, enabling as it does the driver's mood to be assessed at a glance by all other road users, contributes greatly to the elimination of tension. Other drivers, forewarned, can give wide berth to a scowl and even pull into the kerb when confronted with a glower. Such precautions can only help to avoid accidents and thus add a safe element to road conditions, speeding that day of happy accord when all our motorways will be filled with smiling automobiles and their contented drivers.

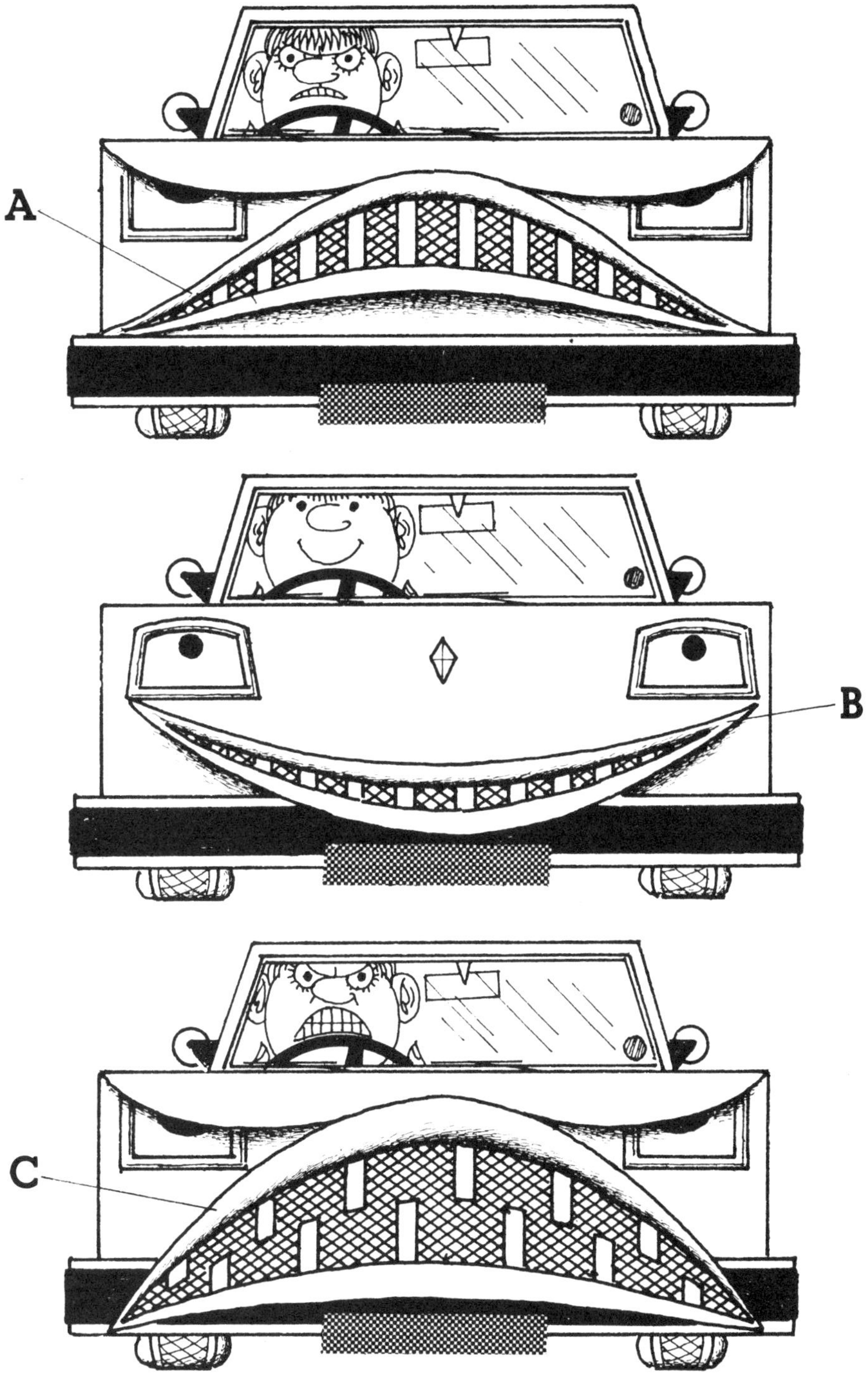
A
B
C

The Lovabike

The hitherto insuperable problem confronting engaged or married couples on tandems has always been that of the rear rider's view. One's loved-one's bottom may or may not be a source of affection, but it is undoubtedly a fact that such a criterion has up to this moment contributed in no small measure to the spate of broken engagements and divorces so prevalent today.

    The Lovabike deals with this problem at a stroke by mounting the lovers face to face. The rider at the rear of the machine is actually in control of steering, braking, etc. For that reason he/she is mounted in a slightly higher position relative to the front rider, over whose head he/she looks while piloting the Lovabike. The pedals are geared together by a crossover chain (A) in such a way that the front rider, though facing backwards, pedals normally. A large mirror (B) is fitted, so that both riders have a forward view.

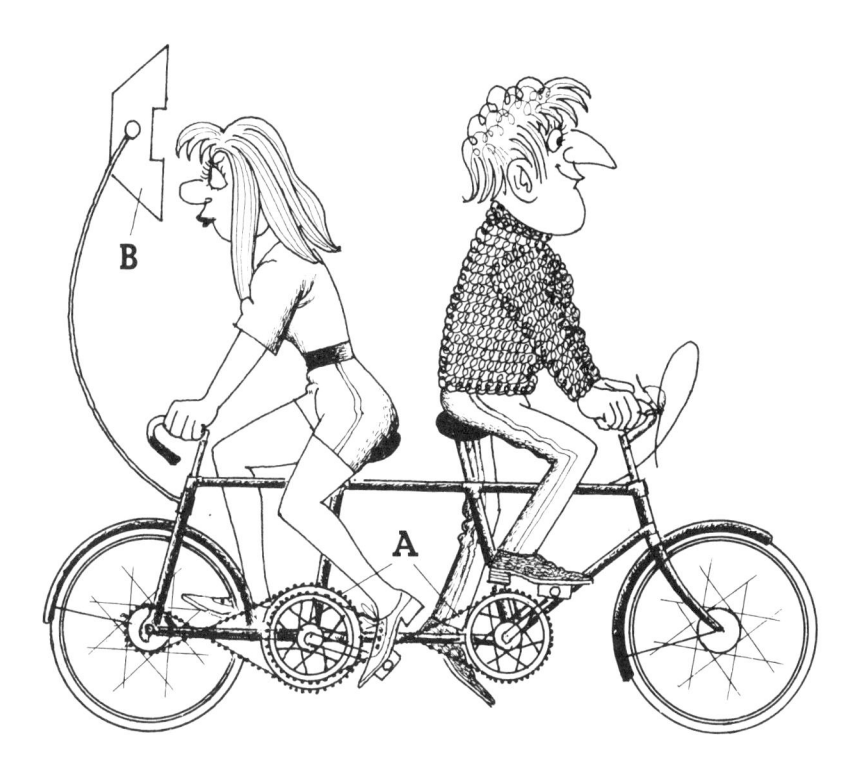

The Tantrum Tandem

Affectionately called the Seven Year Itch machine, the Tantrum Tandem caters effectively for the couple on the verge of estrangement. By eliminating the possibility of conversation leading to quarrels, and also cutting out the 'bottom' view so unavoidably the lot of rear riders on conventional tandems, it may even contribute towards a reconciliation between the two parties.

Either rider may assume the steering position at the front of the vehicle. Suitable crossover gearing (A) ensures that the rearward-facing rider pedals in the manner to which he/she is accustomed, while a periscope (B) enables him/her to see where they are both going.

The Autorek

All the latest and most desirable features are included in the specification of the Autorek, from five-door hatch-back bodywork to reclining seats, automatic gearbox and full airconditioning. It can come in any colour or most colours at once. And, like all cars worthy of the name, it will do 0–60 in 3 seconds and stop in 5, leaving you only 2 seconds to wish you hadn't. And here's the payoff: you don't *need* to waste those 2 precious seconds in wishing you hadn't. For, besides Supazorba seat belts, Squosho upholstery and Instaburp air bags to save you from all possible discomfiture, the Autorek is already designed in a smashed condition.

Mudguards are crumpled; doors bashed in; the windscreen is crazed with cracks; rust appears to be everywhere; and the bumpers, though well and truly fixed, dangle crookedly. Thus, when the passing lorry-driver plunges his vehicle into the side of your new car as it emerges from the showroom, this will only improve its appearance. And after several years' hard battering in city traffic you will have a vehicle of which you can be justly proud.

The advantages of the Autorek are too numerous to mention fully. The social cachet, for example, inherent in the possession of an automobile with your own personalized dents, rather than a mass-produced effort identical with that of your neighbours, cannot be overstressed. And car designers, scorning the need for the retooling of costly presses whenever they intend to produce a new model, will simply aim a heavy blow with a sledge-hammer at a body panel and next year's styling will be with us in its fullest glory.

You may wonder why you shouldn't just visit the local dump and drag out the worst-looking wreck from under the most mangled pile, rather than go to the expense of buying an Autorek. The answer is obvious. The machinery in all Autoreks is of course brand-new when it comes from the manufacturer. And the bodywork, though apparently grievously battered, is fully rustproofed and free from cracks or other faults usually associated with traffic damage. All 'rust' is simulated and the crazing in the windscreen and side windows is carefully placed so as not to obscure visibility. You will have many years' trouble-free motoring with the Autorek, secure in the knowledge that you need never lose your no-claims bonus nor visit costly panel-beaters.

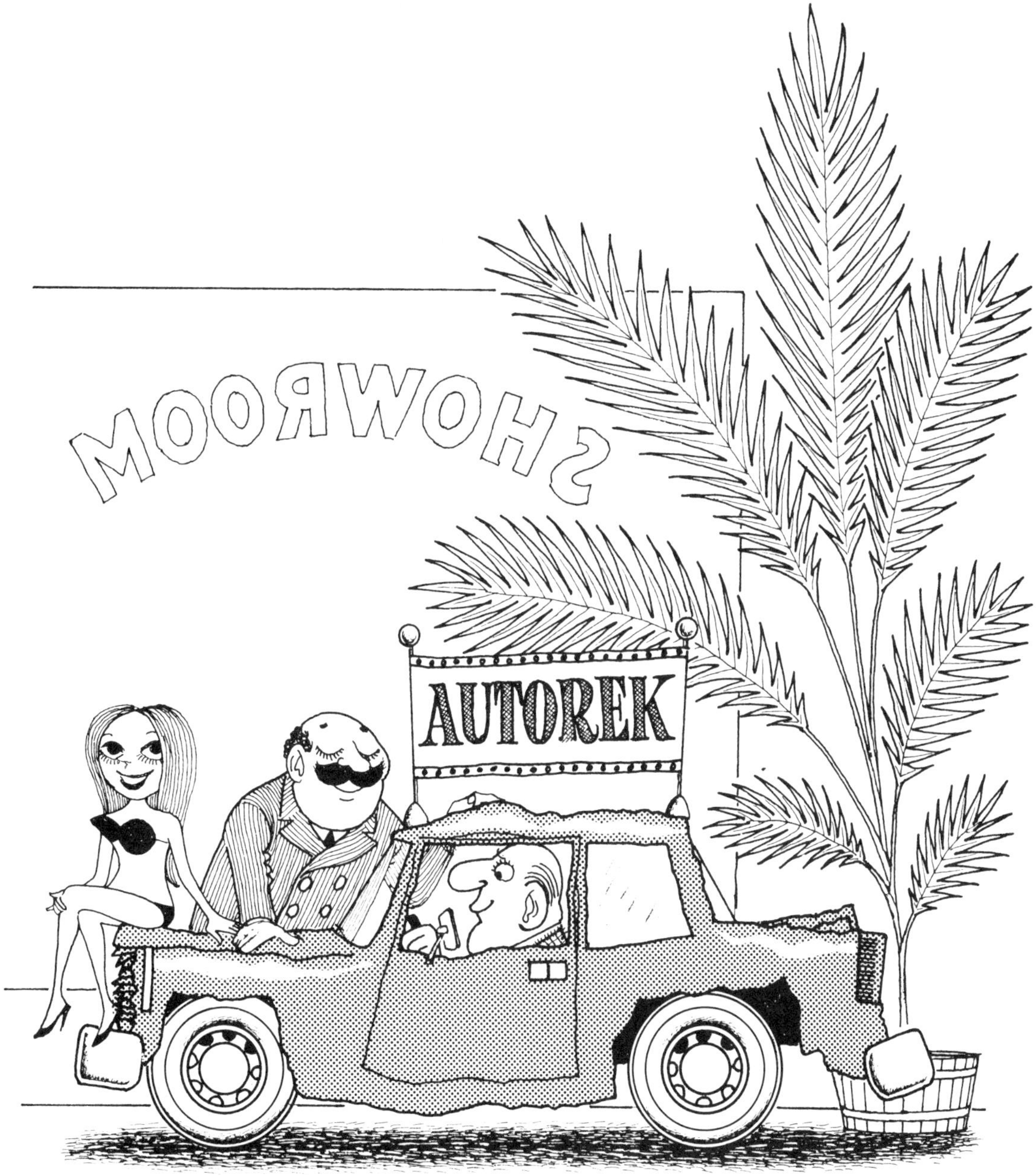
SHOWROOM
AUTOREK

The Meetafeeda

A sophisticated device designed for the affluent, this inserts coins into parking meters at preset intervals. Coins (P) are kept in a mechanical dispenser (Q) which releases them at requisite times (governed by preset clockwork timer (R)) into a tray (S). The weight of the coin on the tray operates a switch (T) which releases a small cloud of smoke (U), effectively hiding the Meetafeeda and meter from the view of suspicious traffic wardens. It also activates a silicon-chip-controlled mechanical hand (V), equipped with a combined magnetic meter sensor and photoelectric eye (W). The hand then swings over towards the tray, grabs the coin and, aligning itself accurately with its sensors as it swings back, thrusts the coin into the meter (X) and winds its key (Y).

GT models are fitted with a second switch (Z), operated when the tray (S) returns to its normal position. This activates an electric motor which rolls the car a few inches forwards or backwards alternately. The vehicle is returned to its original position opposite the parking meter as soon as the second switch (Z) is deactivated. This happens when the next coin is released, depressing the tray again. Because the car has moved between each coin insertion and thus in law is freshly parked, presence of the GT device avoids any possible charge of 'Meter feeding', such as might otherwise be brought by an over-observant traffic warden.

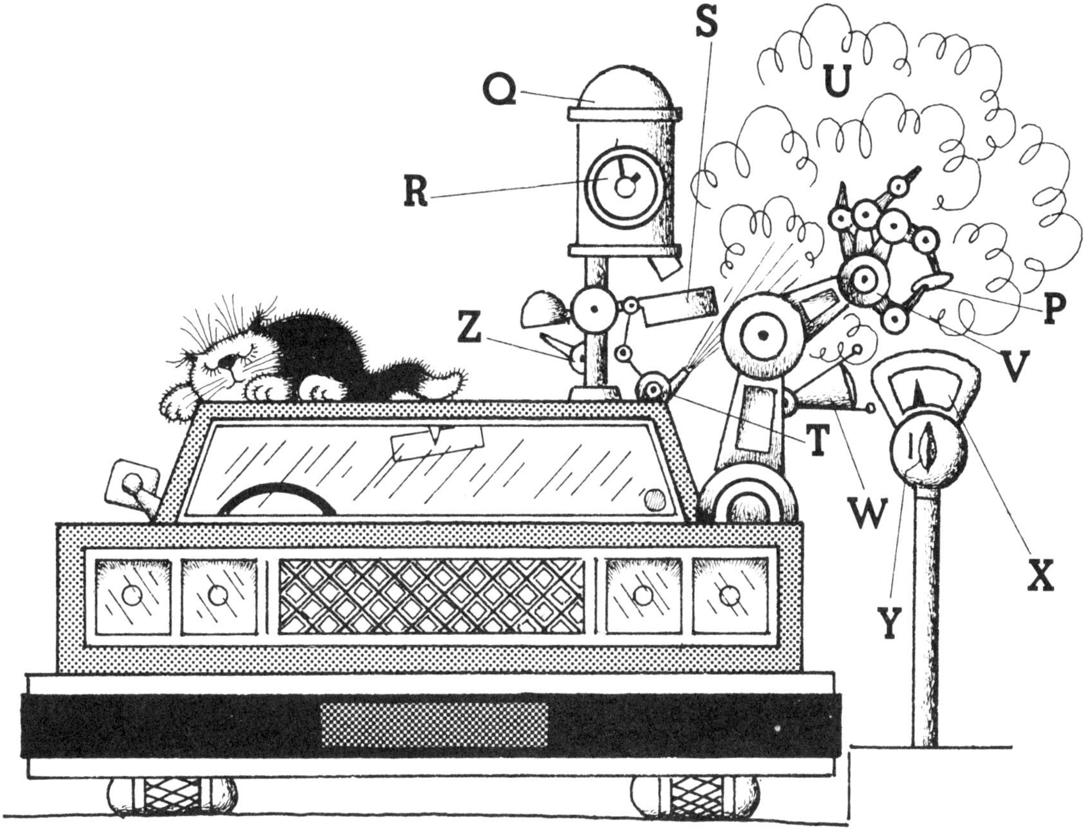
S
Q
U
R
P
Z
V
T
W
X
Y

The Ownameter

A simple but effective device for the thrifty motorist which offers a remarkable degree of immunity from all but the most observant of traffic wardens. In essence it is merely a dummy parking meter (V) with the needle set permanently at 'two hours'. On arrival at a suitable parking place, the driver clamps the meter into a bracket (W) and secures it by a wing-nut (X). On departure he reverses the procedure, unclamping the Ownameter and stowing it in the back of his car. He then folds the bracket (which is hinged at point Y) alongside the mudguard and drives away. A selection of dummy meter-tops (Z) in various styles is provided with this fitment, so that the motorist can still further avoid suspicion by matching his meter to the type used in the district.

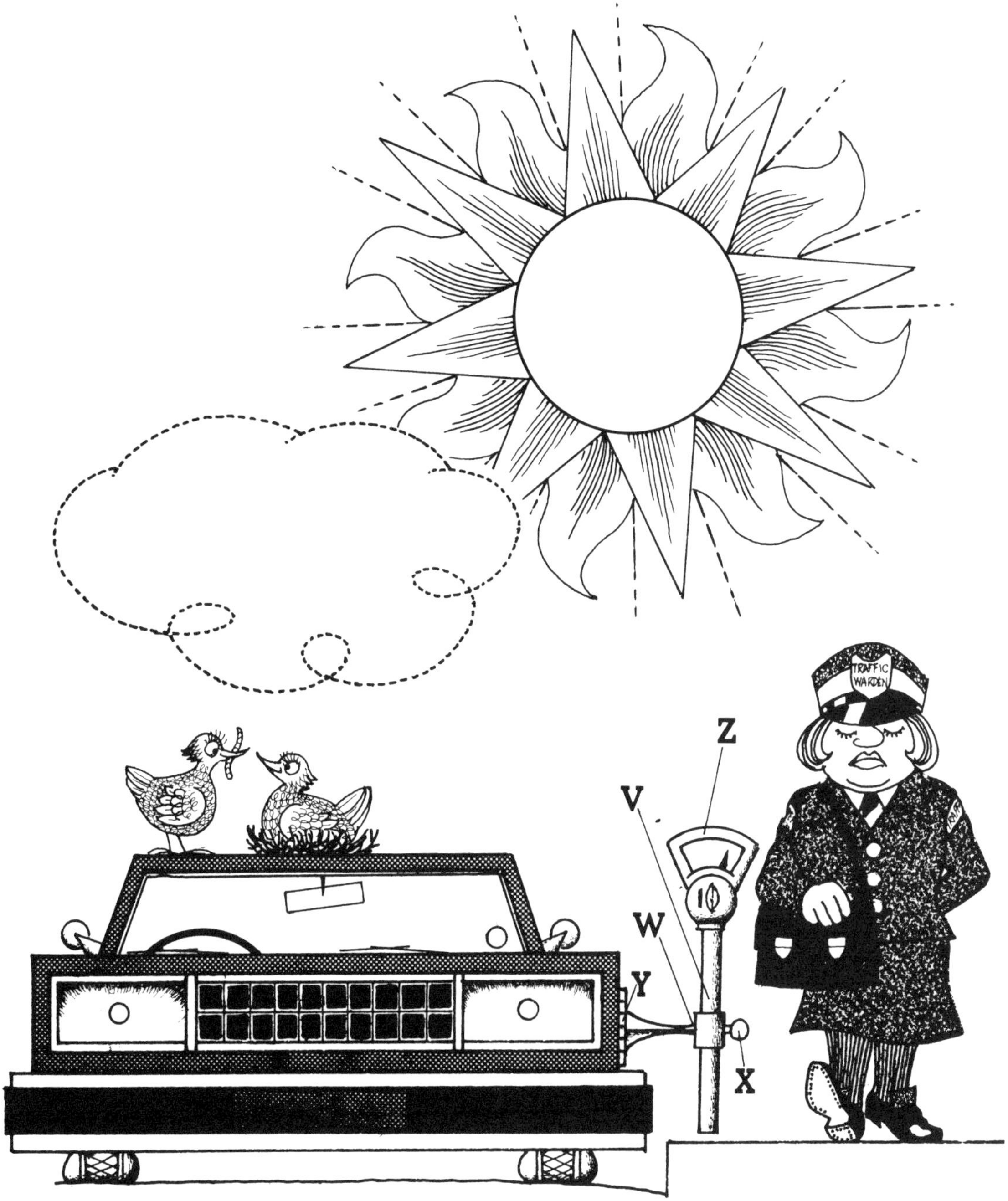
TRAFFIC WARDEN
Z
V
W
Y
X
10

The Philmadent

The invention which will do most to bring down the cost of motor-car comprehensive insurance policies is undoubtedly the Philmadent. This apparatus ensures photographic identification of any vehicle chancing to bump into your unattended car.

The Philmadent consists of a battery-driven cine camera (A) fitted with a wide-angle or fish-eye lens (B) and mounted amidships on top of the car. The camera is set upon a shaft (C) which emerges from a clockwork motor (D). Protruding from the side of the motor is a pin-cam (E), mounted eccentrically on the air-brake shaft (F) of the clockwork motor. This pin-cam is normally arrested by a trembler (G). On top of the cine camera is a governor (H) carrying two flyweights (J and K) which, when in motion, raise the disc (L) by centrifugal force. This disc connects with the trigger of the camera by means of a lever (M).

When the car is bumped from front or rear or either side the Philmadent swings into action. The vibration set up by the bump causes the trembler to quiver, releasing the pin-cam and allowing the clockwork motor to run. This in turn rotates the cine camera, causing the governor to throw out its flyweights, thus raising the disc and moving the lever. The camera is then set in operation.

It will quickly be seen that the revolving cine camera aided by its fish-eye lens, will rapidly photograph all objects in the immediate vicinity, including the number plate of the offending vehicle. Conclusive and irrefutable evidence is then available which will ensure that any damage is paid for by its perpetrator. When the car stops vibrating the trembler will cease to quiver and return to its quiescent position, arresting the motion of the clockwork motor by blocking once again the rotation of the pin-cam. The centrifugal force affecting the flyweights will then cease, the disc will drop, the lever will return to its original position, and the camera will stop running. This saves film, ready for the next bump.

When the car is to be driven normally, the Philmadent is immobilized by a bell crank (N) which, moved aside automatically when the driver opens his door, acts as a 'steady' to the trembler and prevents its quivering.

BONK!

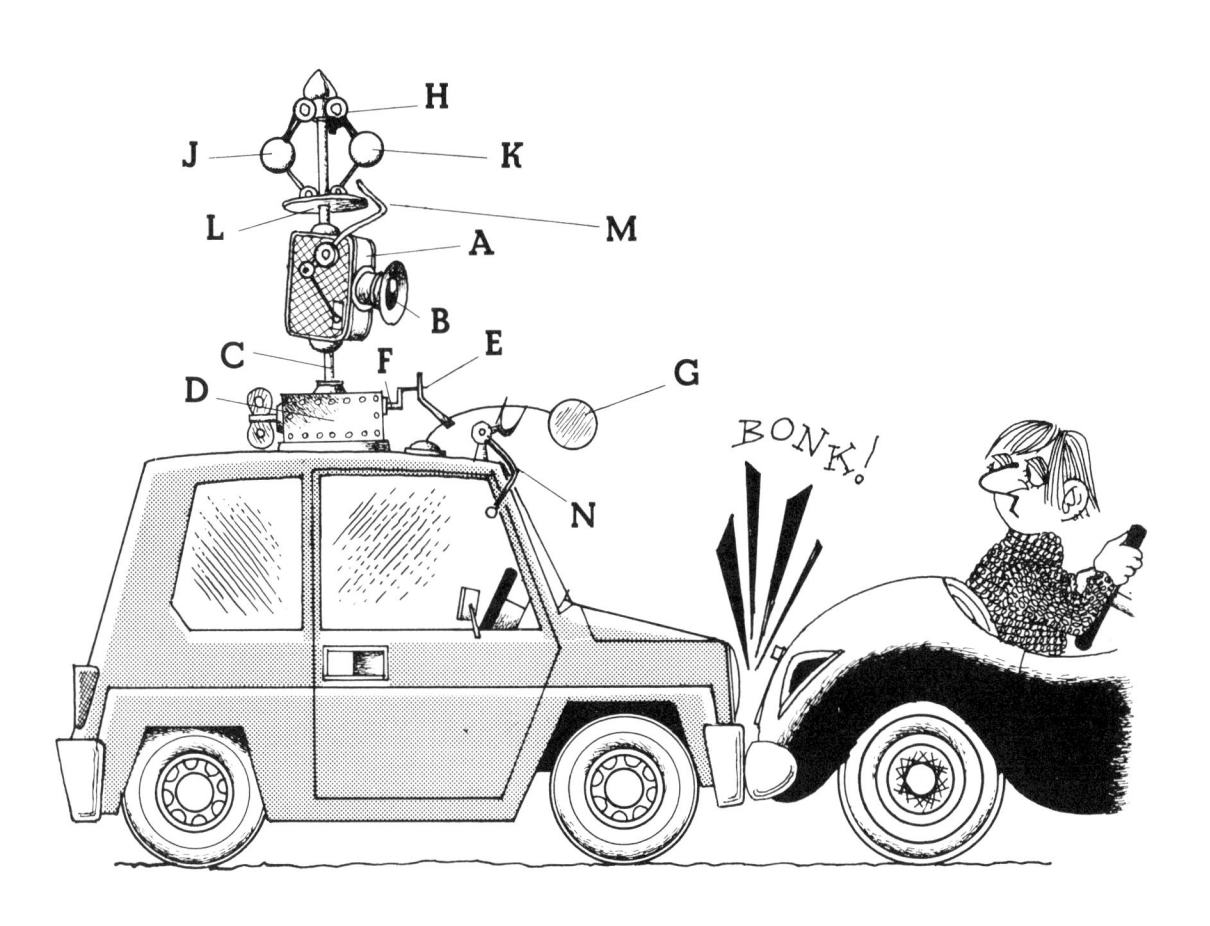

The Hikycle

Setting aside the return to the horse as too Utopian, the bicycle offers a possible solution to many if not all of the problems of our modern motor car culture: over-congestion on the roads, parking impossibilities, atmospheric pollution, and the motorist's general lack of physical fitness. The bicycle is cheap, handy and health-giving, and creates no noisome fumes to pollute the air. There is, however, one large problem which inhibits its universal adoption. With the exception of Holland, and perhaps Sweden, no country has taken the trouble to provide the bicycle and its rider with enough protection from yet another of the motor car's side-effects: its efficiency as a lethal projectile.

For the average bicyclist the pavement offers a tempting alternative to dicing with death on the road, but the trouble here is that archaic laws, still in force in many parts of the world, forbid the riding of bicycles thereupon. Hence the Hikycle. By employing boots instead of tyres it overcomes certain aspects of the law, for surely if a pavement is not available for boots and shoes to walk upon, what on earth *is* it for?

The Hikycle can come in various forms to suit the uses to which it is likely to be put. For example, if it is to spend much time on muddy unmade roads, or even crossing fields, spiked boots will ensure maximum traction and grip, while running shoes on a racing Hikycle are an obvious modification. Fashionable shoes on women's Hikycles would impart a touch of style in the smarter areas of our cities. The footwear industry, too, would benefit, adding a welcome stimulus to the prosperity of our high street traders.

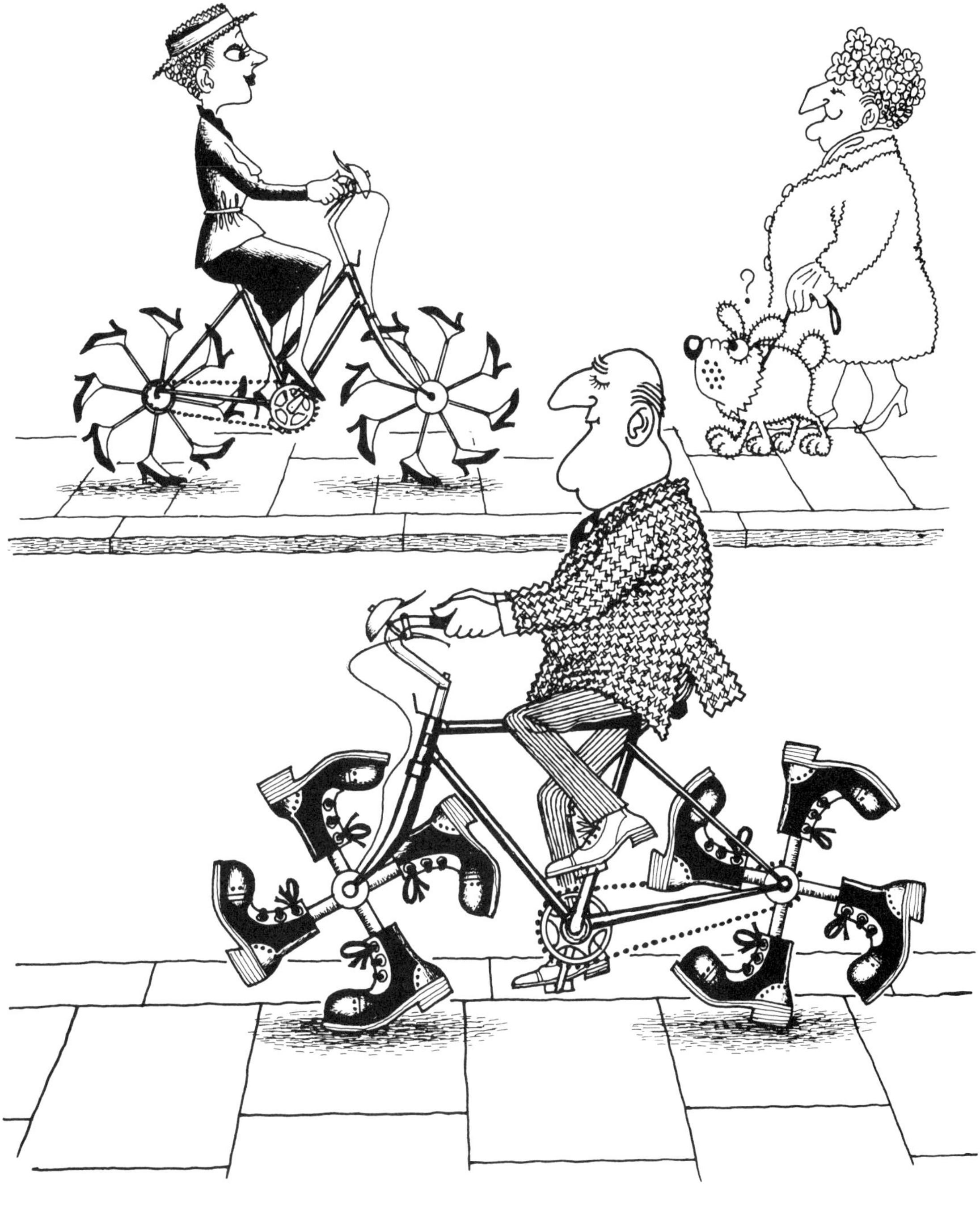

The Microcar

For many years there has been an urgent need for a really small vehicle, expressly designed with commuter transport in mind. Until the invention of the Microcar, however, the associated problem of prestige preservation has remained elusive of solution. Company directors, senior executives and most members of the Government, accustomed to travelling in Rolls-Royces, Mercedes and Cadillacs, have been reluctant to be seen, even dead, on bicycles or mopeds, up till now the only alternative form of transport available providing the economy in petrol and space that is so urgently required.

The Microcar is a minute four-wheeled automobile, designed as an exact replica of the company director's principal prestige vehicle, even to the registration number and colour scheme. Custom and advertising will rapidly establish this identification in the public mind, ensuring that no loss of respect, deference or admiration will be experienced by the VIP when he is driving his Microcar.

A comfortable seat (A) and steering wheel (B), both mounted telescopically, are provided. These can be released by means of wing-nuts (G), and will slide down into the body of the car and be covered by lids (H) when off the road. A convenient handle (C) between the accelerator and brake pedal makes the vehicle readily transportable by hand. It thus takes up little more room than a suitcase and can be carried into restaurants, theatres, clubs and other places of entertainment.

An umbrella (E) can be clamped on the steering wheel by means of a clip (D). Another umbrella (F) serves as a gear lever. Experience has shown that, particularly in the case of the Microcar, a spare umbrella is far more useful than a spare wheel as, in the event of a flat tyre, it can easily be carried home. A clip-on rear-view mirror is standard equipment. This clamps to the VIP's hat brim and can be placed in his pocket on arrival at his destination.

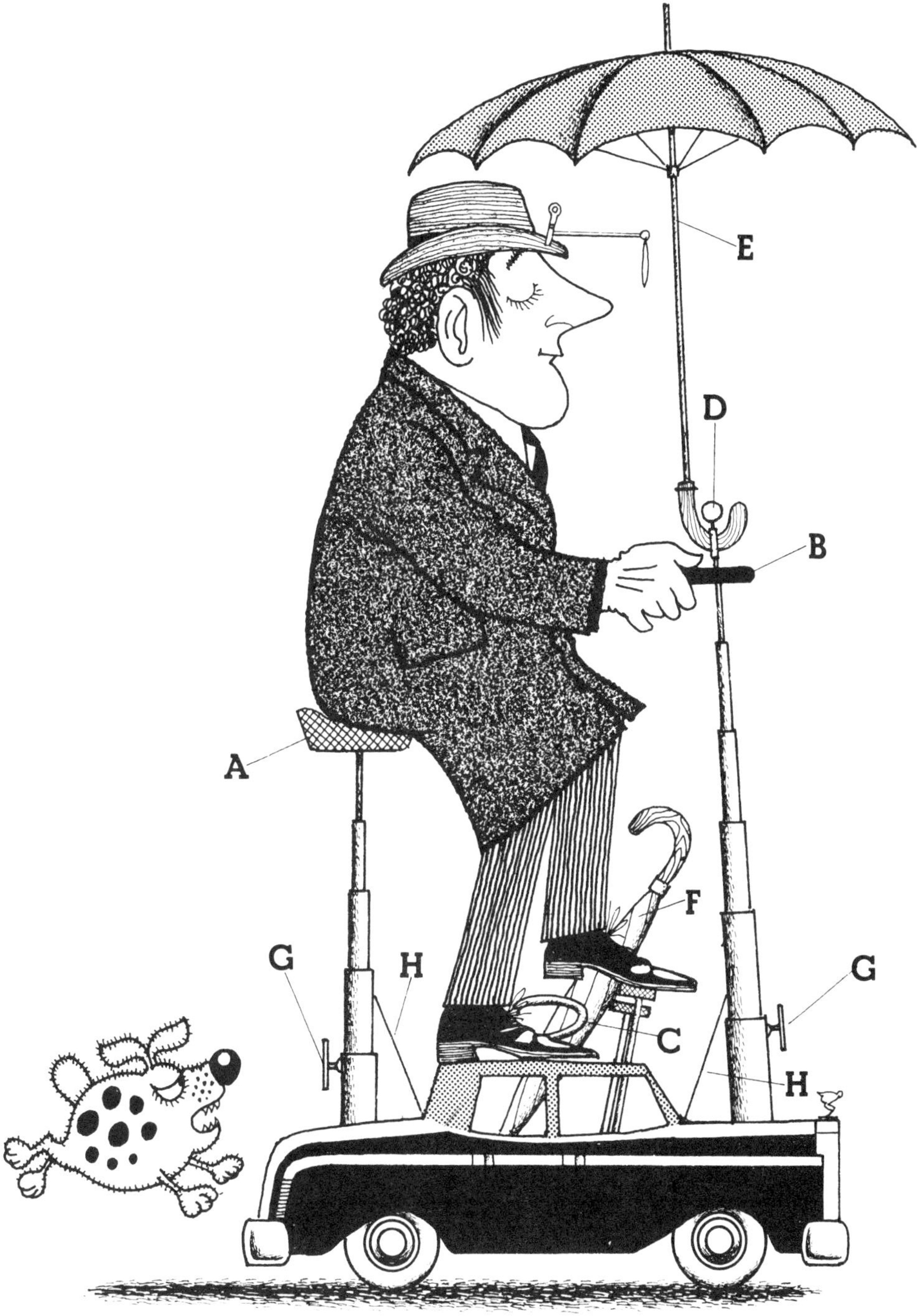
E
D
B
A
F
G
H
C
H
G

The Savaspace

The Savaspace is basically a crane or hoist (A), erected on the wall of the car-owner's house, from which is suspended a one-ton weight (B), suitably inscribed so that no road user can be unaware of its nature. Besides intimations of its weight, boldly lettered on all four sides, there is an inscription on the base which announces that it will descend abruptly and unexpectedly at unspecified intervals.

Although the one-ton weight is normally suspended (as illustrated), let us suppose, for the purpose of simplifying the description of the operation sequence, that it is at rest upon the street below. The apparatus is activated by a keyswitch (C), thus energizing the electric motor (D) which slowly winds up the weight to its 'menace' position (E). At this point the contact (F) meets with a bellcrank (G) which turns off a switch (H), stopping the motor. While this is happening the ratchet-wheel (J) is revolving with the winding drum (K) and the check-pawl (L) is riding over the ratchets, like the 'click' of a clock being wound.

At the opposite end of the pawl, past the fulcrum, is a bucket (M), empty at this phase of the operation. A tap (N), situated outside a window higher up the house wall, is set to drip at a prearranged rate, slowly filling the bucket. When the weight of water in the bucket reaches a certain value, the pawl is withdrawn, the bucket descends, a trip (O) catches upon a bracket (P), the bucket overturns and the water is discharged, incidentally watering the garden below. Meanwhile the one-ton weight, released from the retaining pawl, descends rapidly to street level. At this point the contact reaches the lever (Q) which moves, pulling back the bellcrank via a chain (R) riding over a pulley (S). This raises a rod (T), starting the electric motor again by activating the switch (H) and recommencing the cycle. Meanwhile the bucket, now empty of water, rises to its original position, re-engaging the pawl with the ratchet wheel.

When the owner of the Savaspace wishes to park his own vehicle outside his house he simply operates the keyswitch which cuts off the electric current and turns off the water supply to the tap. This arrests the impending descent of the weight, which remains suspended until reanimated by a second insertion of the key. The owner can thus safely park his car under the weight. An umbrella over the bucket ensures that rainwater cannot enter it and trigger the mechanism accidentally.

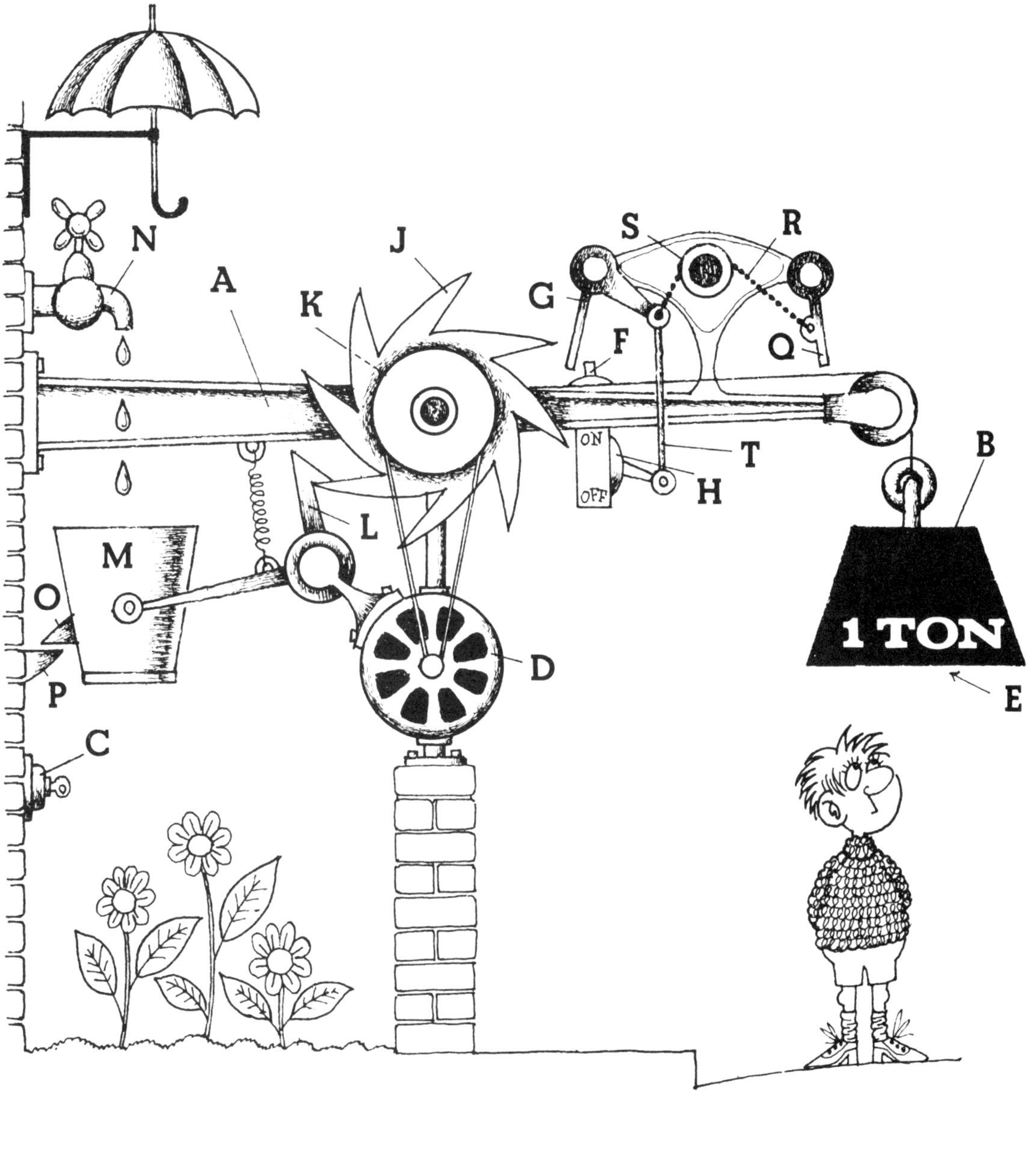

N
A
J
K
S
R
G
F
Q
ON
OFF
T
H
B
L
M
O
P
1 TON
D
E
C

The Outline

All motorists suffer from the unimaginative activities of city councils, aided and abetted by their governments, who place great importance on the manufacture of the motor car as a means of providing employment and export trade, and then go to inordinate lengths to ensure that there is nowhere for their products to be parked. Thus most of our cities and towns are festooned with unsightly yellow lines painted in the gullies alongside the pavement kerbstones. Sometimes the lines are double and quite often reinforced by yellow daubs painted on the kerbstones as well. But the presence of even a smidgin of yellow paint means only one thing: You May Not Park Here and If You Do You Will Be Towed Away and Have to Pay A Hell Of A Fine.

The Outline does the only sensible thing with these anti-parking lines: It eliminates them. A tank of tar (A) is mounted on the roof-rack. A pipe (B), with control valve (C), emerges from this tank and leads down to a point just behind the rear wheel. A second pipe (D) leads from the end of the exhaust pipe, discharging under the tar tank. When the vehicle is in motion heat from the exhaust warms and liquefies the tar in the tank (and for good measure dispels the exhaust gases harmlessly in the air instead of blasting them into the heater intake of the car behind). Just before parking, the driver pulls down the lever controlling valve C, which permits liquid tar to flow down pipe B. He then reverses his vehicle in to his chosen parking space, while the rear tyre, acting like a printer's inking roller, squeezes hot tar over the anti-parking line and obliterates it.

In our illustration the discerning reader will observe that the Outline is being parked on the offside of the road, whereas the normal procedure is to park on the nearside. At a slight extra charge the Outline can be equipped for easy nearside parking. In this case the pipe (B) discharges behind the nearside rear wheel, and a suitable mirror is supplied which enables the driver to observe the operation from the driver's seat.

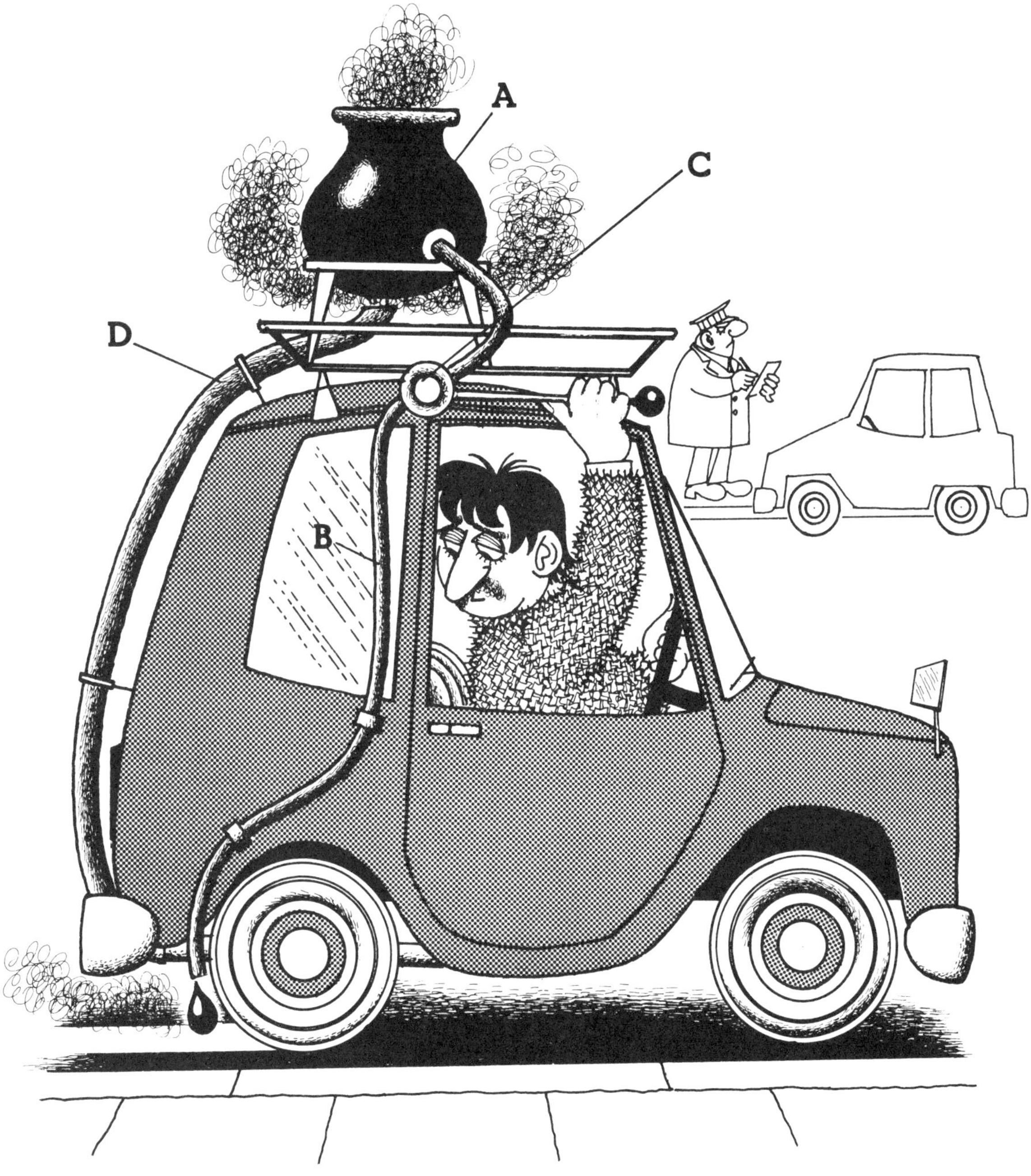
A
C
D
B

The Entertail

Every day throughout the Western world, an infinity of man-hours is being frittered away by legions of bored motorists, forever contemplating the often unattractive rear-ends of the stationary automobiles immediately in front of them. And yet, during all this time, large sums of money could be pouring into the coffers of advertising agents, movie makers, television companies and other moguls of the entertainment and publicity world.

A video screen (A) fixed to the tail of your car, that is all that is needed—at once improving its appearance and providing a source of revenue. Projecting from the rear of the Entertail-equipped car is a flexible, telescopic boom (B), rather like a fishing rod, at the end of which is a coin collector (C). Within easy reach of the driver is a video player and a supply of tapes. As soon as a promising traffic jam develops the Entertail operator displays upon his rear screen a slide carrying a list of available video-recorded films marked in order, say, from 1 to 10, with instructions to the following driver asking him to hoot the number of the film he wants. Other instructions request him to place the requisite number of coins in the collector, now dangling by his window. As soon as the coins are inserted the chosen video-tape is inserted and the performance commences, whiling away the time in the pleasantest way possible for the driver behind whilst earning money for the one in front.

If the invitation to choose and pay for entertainment elicits no response, such as may well be the case if the age of the following vehicle suggests an impecunious driver, the Entertail operator puts his second money-spinner into operation, by running a sequence of advertisements. A digital counter records the number of times these advertisements are projected, so that the advertising agent can pay the Entertail operator accordingly. The driver behind is persuaded into buying some product that he didn't know he wanted, trade is stimulated—and the country prospers.

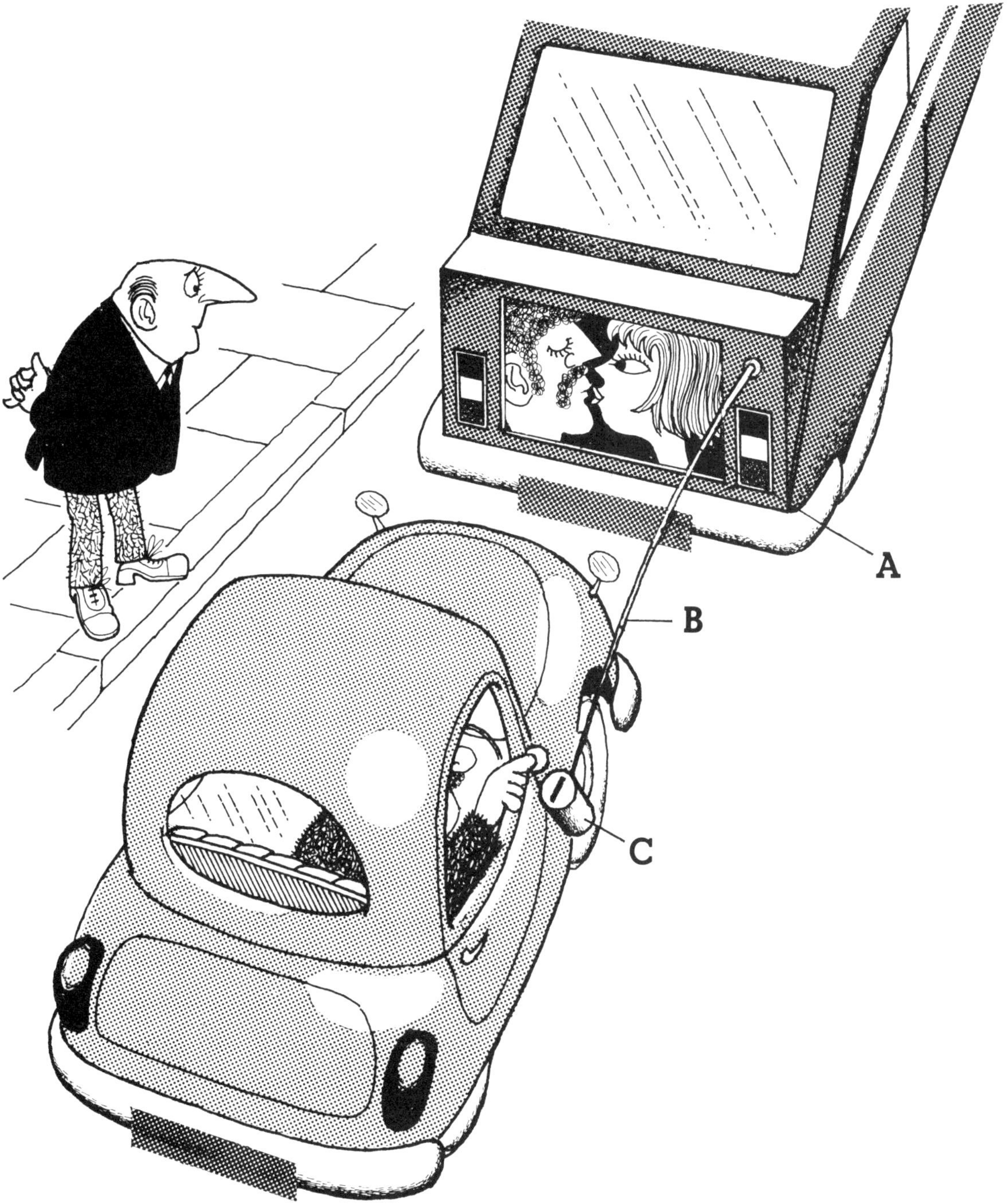
A
B
C

The Prodomat

Instead of imposing heavy fines and long prison sentences, courts will turn increasingly to the Prodomat as a deterrent to the dangerous or careless driver. Furthermore, insurance companies will soon insist on their installation as a fairer method of penalizing the dent-prone motorist without raising the premiums of the innocent.

The Prodomat consists of a framework of pins (A) surrounding the driver and aimed at different parts of his anatomy. Each pin is connected to a solenoid (B) and each corresponds to a like part of the vehicle, for example (C), wired to its associated solenoid by electric cable and contact switches. In use, any part of the car bumped either accidentally or through carelessness causes the associated contact switch to operate, triggering its related solenoid and thus inserting or prodding its pin into the driver's person at a point corresponding to the affected area of the car.

A first offender might be sentenced to compulsory installation for, say, six months. Persistent wrongdoers could be equipped for life—at their own expense of course. On the other hand, careful drivers could opt for voluntary installation, with corresponding reduction of insurance premium and perhaps the bestowment of some State honour, such as a medal carrying two life-preservers on an azure ground, with bar.

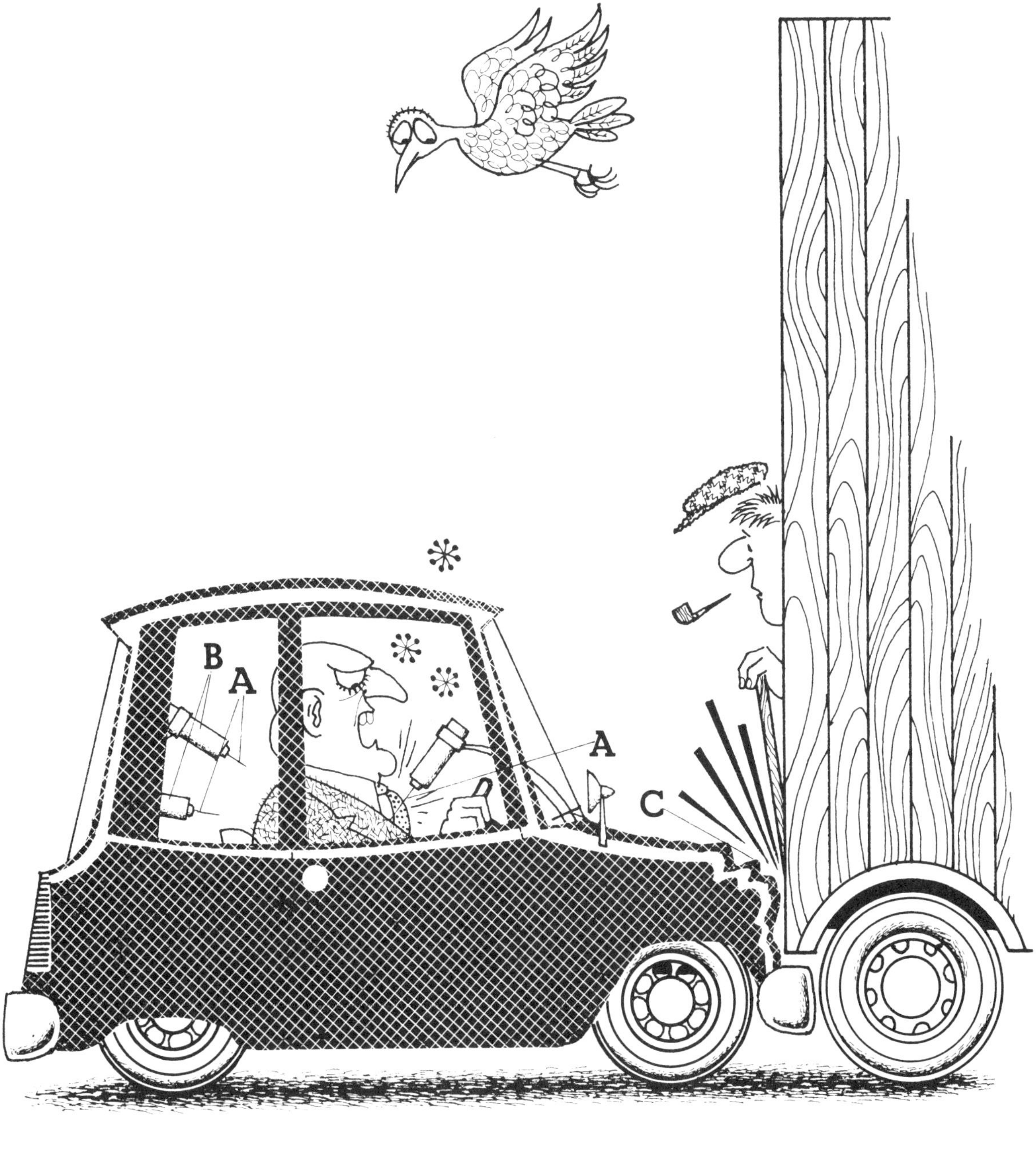
B
A
A
C

The Autohole

The Autohole is a car constructed to resemble a road-repair equipage, complete with roadman's (driving) hut (A) and 'tea and tool' cabin (B) for passengers. It may normally be parked anywhere, including Piccadilly Circus or in the middle of a motorway, without exciting any interest. When in motion the 'Road Up' sign is replaced by a number plate. Where police and traffic wardens are particularly pernickety, additional immunity is provided by plastic simulated sand-heaps (C) which, placed over the road-wheels, eliminate the only weak spot in an otherwise impenetrable disguise.

ROAD UP

The Clockar

Alternatives to the petrol engine as a method of powering motor cars have been sought for many years. Back in the nineties of the last century steam and electricity were both tried, with considerable success. But the problem with steam was the raising of it, and electric cars have always had only a short mileage range, after which they have to be pushed home.

The Clockar solves these problems in the simplest way by employing the age-old and well-tried clockwork motor. This has great advantages over the electric car. For example it carries no heavy short-lived battery. It can also be rewound quickly. In order to exploit fully this particular virtue, the Clockar is fitted with a large rubber sucker (A) mounted on the front of the vehicle. A small bell mounted near the driver warns when the spring is approaching the point of run-down. The driver then gets behind, and drives up to, the rear of the nearest bus, or any other vehicle with a flat rear panel (B), such as a delivery truck, and pushes the sucker against it. He then jams on his brakes and the sucker is pulled away from the Clockar, unreeling a cord (C) attached to the winding mechanism. When the cord is fully extended the sucker is pulled off the back of the bus and the cord, with sucker attached, is rapidly wound back into the Clockar by a small return spring. The Clockar is now fully powered and can proceed on its way.

An additional re-powering device is incorporated. This is the so-called 'inertia pedal' and takes the place of the brake in a conventional vehicle. When the Clockar descends a hill, or decelerates rapidly, the inertia pedal engages the winding mechanism, slowing the car and restoring power to the driving spring at the same time. In addition to these features every Clockar owner has an electrically-driven winding device fixed to the end of his garage. This engages with a large key (D) on the front of the Clockar.

As the Clockar becomes established, public authorities, ever watchful for ways of making more money from motorists, will fit winding devices (E) to parking meters (F), charging a fee sufficient to cover parking and electricity for winding. Filling stations will follow suit with winding pumps instead of, or as well as, the petrol variety. And in an emergency the driver himself can give a few turns to the key, thus providing power enough to get him home, with a bout of healthful exercise into the bargain.

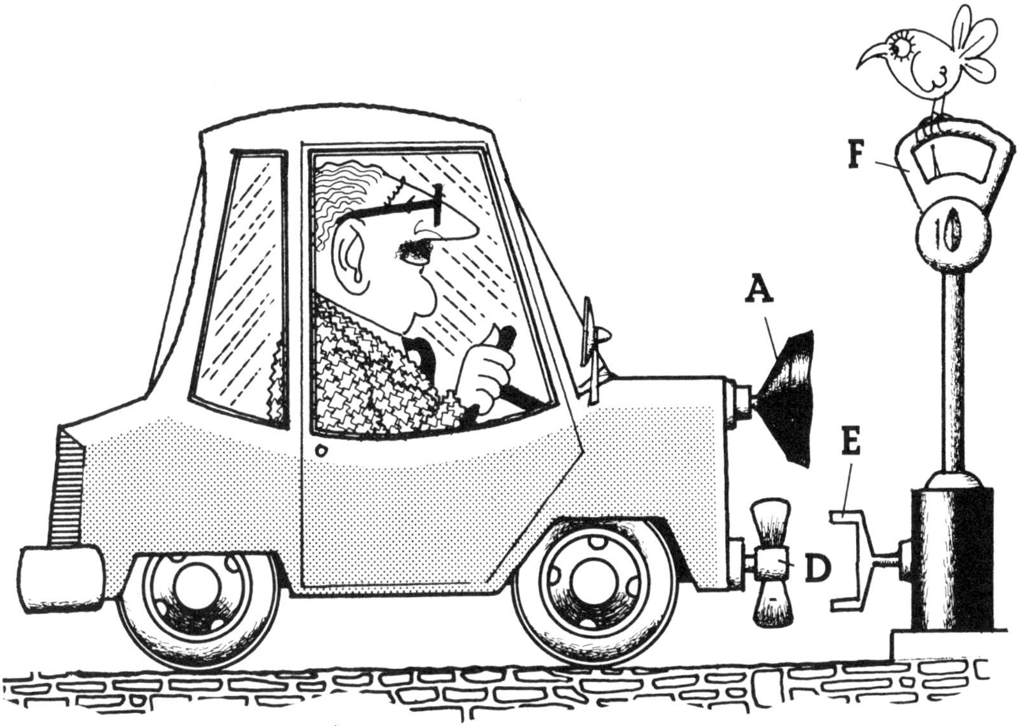
A
F
10
E
D

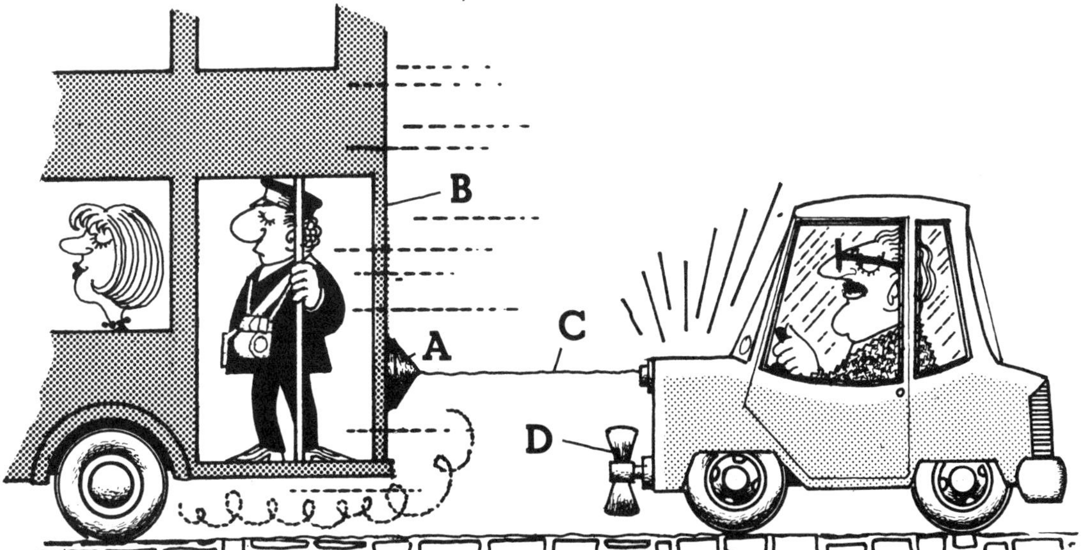
B
A
C
D

The Ballooter

To the owner of a Ballooter the nightmare miseries of the rush hour are a distant memory. At 8 a.m. each morning he cranks up the tiny motorcycle engine (G), takes his seat over the petrol tank (H) and steps on the pedal (J). This releases lighter-than-air helium gas, kept under pressure in a tank (K), via a valve (L), pump/bypass valve (T) and pipe (M), to a balloon gas-bag (N) kept folded when deflated in a tray (O). As the gas-bag fills the Ballooter rises into the air, its engine idling gently. At the required height the commuter eases his foot on the pedal (J), takes the rudder-bar (P) in his left hand and depresses the accelerator pedal (Q). The propeller (R) speeds up and the Ballooter moves off in the direction of the commuter's place of work. He can now relax and read his morning newspaper, occasionally glancing down to see where he is. On approaching his office he decelerates and takes his foot off the pedal (J). In this position the pump (S) is activated by a valve (T) and, driven by the now idling engine, it draws helium from the balloon and pumps it back into the tank (K). The gas-bag deflates and the Ballooter sinks gently to the pavement.

As the engine is coupled to roadwheels (U) via chain and clutch (V), the commuter may traverse the last few yards still under power, steering the vehicle by a castor-wheel (W) coupled to the rudder (X) by a bar (Y). Finally, he alights from the machine, switches off the engine and, pausing only to fold the deflated gas-bag into its tray, wheels the Ballooter into its parking place by pushing on its handle (Z).

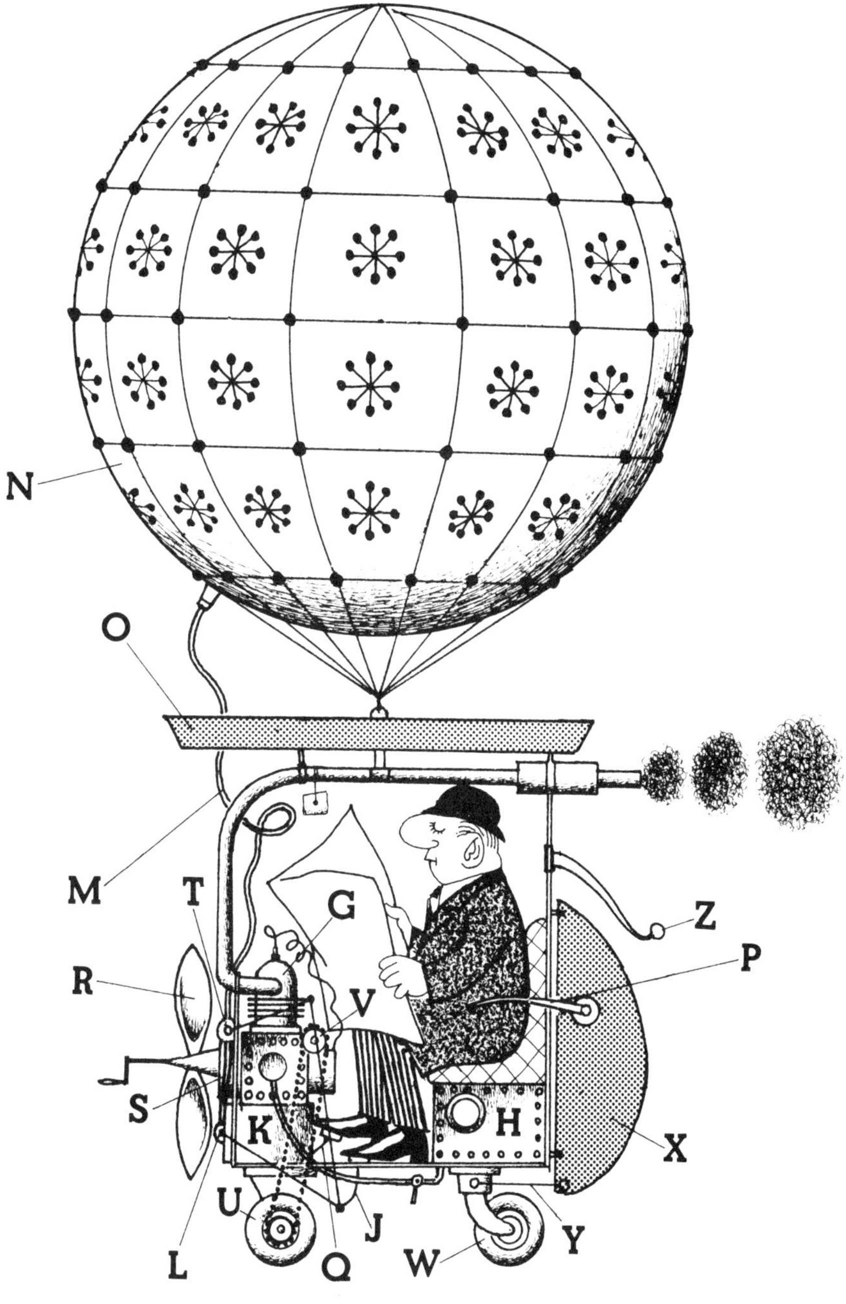
N
O
M
T
G
Z
P
R
V
S
K
H
X
U
J
Y
L
Q
W

The Economicar

The Economicar is a very lightly-built vehicle, conceived to take advantage of every available power-source, except that supplied by petrol. For example, the interior is fitted with saddles and pedals (A), one set for each occupant, so that power output automatically increases with the passenger load. Additional saddles and pedals are fitted to each of the four wheels, enabling extra people to be carried, small detachable umbrellas (B) sheltering them from the elements.

On the roof of the Economicar is a bath-shaped tank (C) for use in wet weather. Rain collecting in the tank is piped (D) to a waterwheel (E) which, though not powerful enough in itself to supply sufficient motive force, helps the pedallers in their work. Solar panels (F) provide power to an electric motor (in G), which can also assist in the generation of motive force when the weather is fine.

Fixed to the roof is a trolley pole (H), useful in towns where trams run. A negative contact (J) is provided to complete the current through the tram rails. Power from this source is fed into the electric motor, providing ample energy to shift the heaviest loads. In the absence of trams, the pole may be locked in an upright position and a sail (K) attached. This again can furnish adequate power when the wind is in the right direction.

The front steering arrangement is on the horse-and-buggy principle, i.e. the entire front axle swings on a central pivot (L). This arrangement is adopted so that, should a horse be available, the vehicle can be pulled by it, via shafts (M) attached to the front bogie (N). Linking the shafts at the front end is a detachable cross-bar carrying in its centre a combined trailer socket and grapnel (O). By this means the shafts can be hooked on to any suitable passing vehicle.

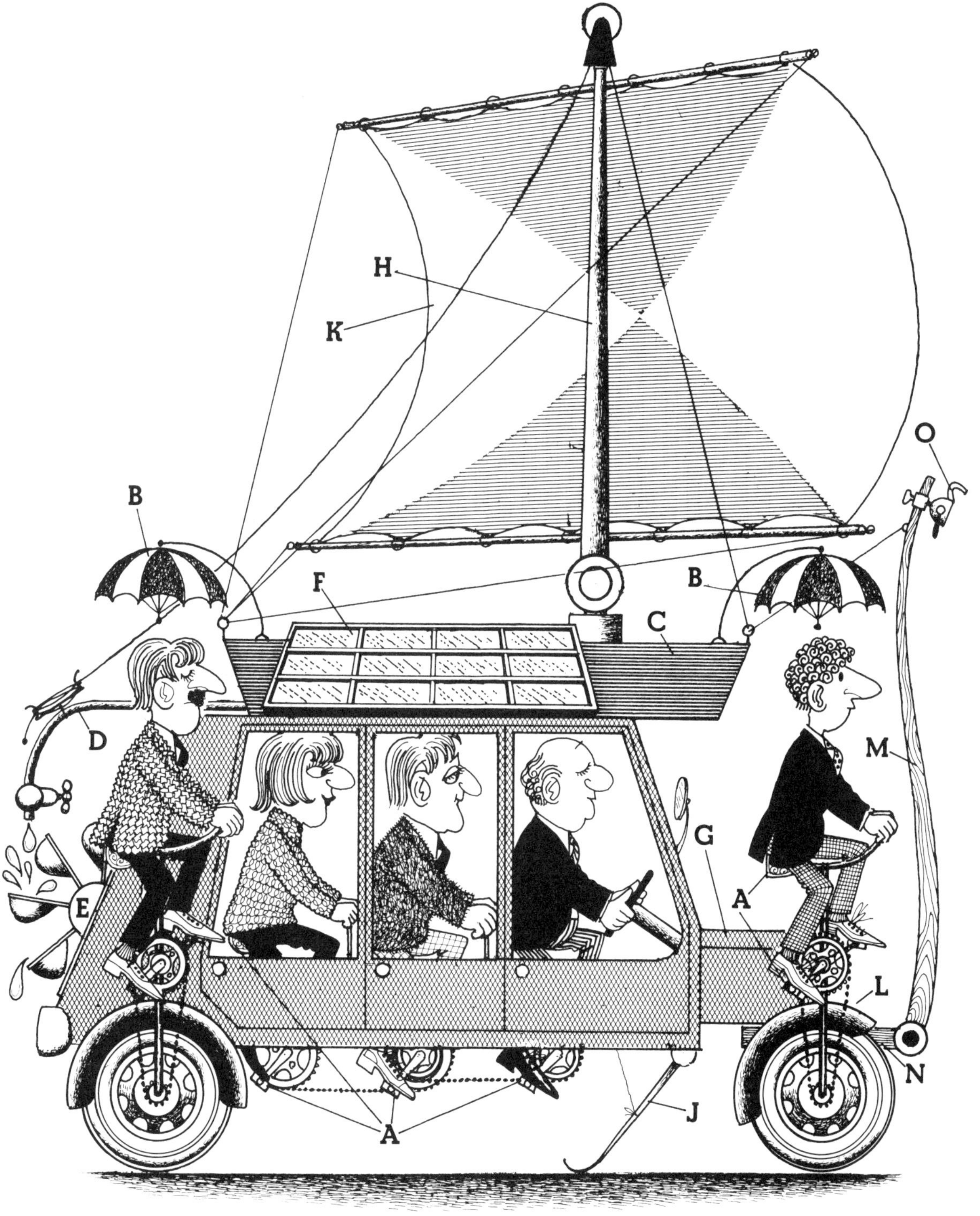
H
K
B
B
F
C
D
E
G
A
A
L
M
N
O
J
A

The Nonag

The mother-in-law/back-seat driver joke has been with us for so long that the anguish and passionate emotions lying behind it have tended to become obscured. A close friend of the author has had much experience of this particular syndrome. In earlier days, he says, this was supplied by his mother, who used to emit shrill gasps of horror when confronted with an emergency as mild as that of a cat crossing the road a quarter of a mile ahead.

Latterly his mother's shrieks of fear have been replaced by the expostulations of a much younger lady, who resolutely refuses to believe that anyone but herself is capable even of starting the engine, let alone of being equipped with enough common sense and judgment to operate the steering wheel, accelerator and brake in a manner conducive to the avoidance of accidents. The resulting torrent of abuse, expletives and remonstration (A), delivered at high volume and with few pauses for breath, whenever the luckless gentleman dares to occupy the driver's seat even in the emptiest of country lanes, has caused him long ago to relinquish all control of the vehicle to his lady friend's unadventurous but modestly capable hands.

The staggeringly simple Nonag solves the problem of the back-seat driver on the 'if you can't beat 'em, join 'em' principle, by transferring all controls to the back seat (B). The front seat of the Nonag is arranged in a reclining position (C) so that the ex-driver can doze comfortably and the back-seat driver can see over his head. Further to facilitate visibility, the back-seat driver's seat is elevated slightly. Steering is transmitted to the front wheels by indirect gearing (at D). This avoids any inconvenience to the ex-driver in front, such as might be caused by the conventional steering column.

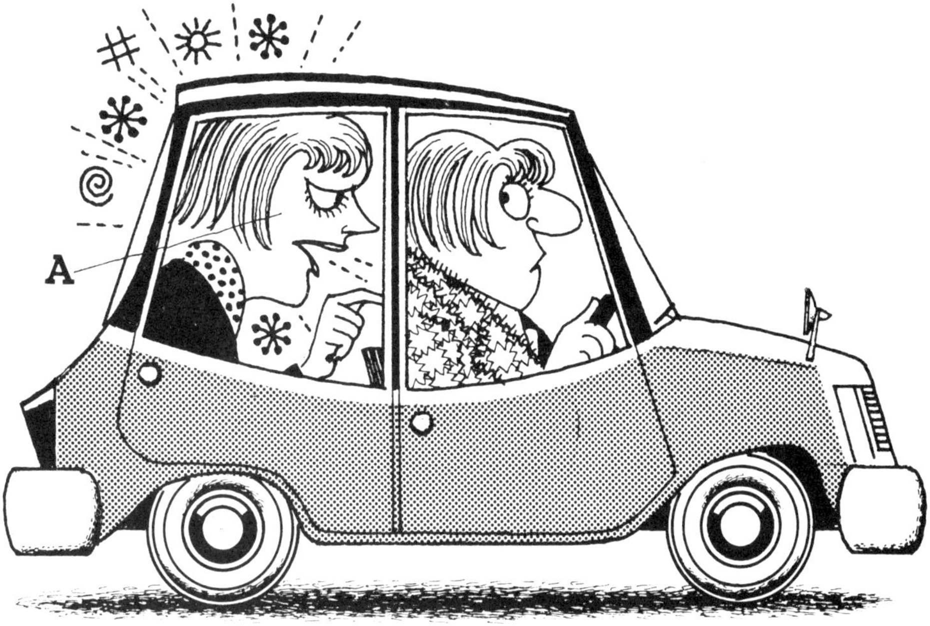
A

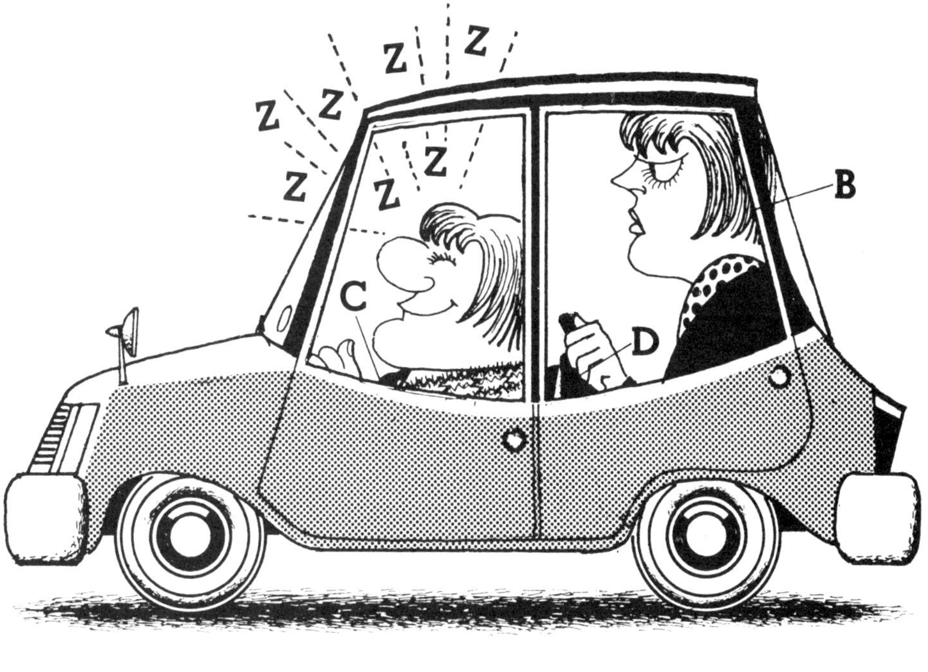
Z Z Z Z Z Z Z
B
C
D

The Jamhopper

The Jamhopper is equipped with a facility never before fitted to an automobile, though the need for it has been self-evident for many decades. This facility, effected by a very specialized suspension system, consists of a self-elevating mechanism which enables the Jamhopper to rise above surrounding traffic and in fact ride over it.

When the Jamhopper is in its normal position it is almost indistinguishable from a conventional mini-bus type car. However, the vehicle is somewhat wider than average, and close inspection reveals the presence of forks (A), like those on a bicycle, holding each wheel. On pulling a lever the driver can elevate the car to a height sufficient to clear the roofs of other vehicles, over which he may then drive, the extra width enabling the Jamhopper to straddle other road users without difficulty. Miles of stationary traffic can thus be negotiated with almost as much ease as if the road were empty.

The elevation of the front end is achieved by telescopic legs (B) operated by air pressure from a compressor pump. These legs are mounted vertically so that steering can be transmitted via them to the wheels. The rear of the Jamhopper is raised by a slightly different method, as motive power has to be supplied to the back wheels and this might lead to instability if transmitted through vertical legs. Instead, hollow swinging arms (C) are pivoted at the front of the vehicle. Through these arms run propeller shafts geared separately to each rear wheel and driven from a transverse drive-axle/differential at (D). Telescopic arms (E) apply the elevating facility from the same compressor pump.

It is worth bearing in mind when driving a Jamhopper that, should you happen to pass over a container, or other flat-topped truck which is travelling at a reasonable speed in spite of the traffic, you can lower the car on to it, thus hitching a lift with consequent large savings in fuel. A careful watch, however, should always be kept for bridges.

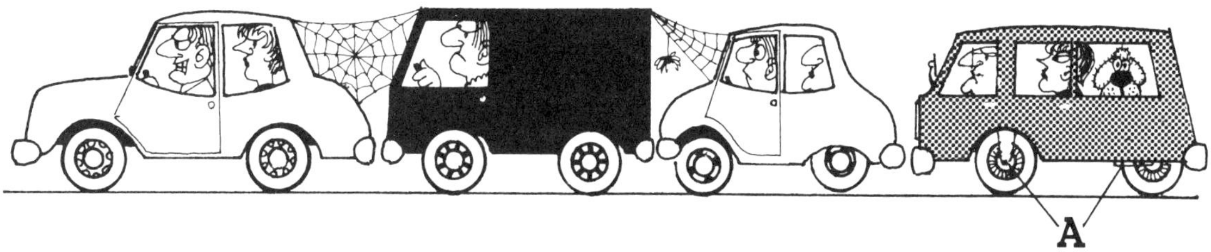
A

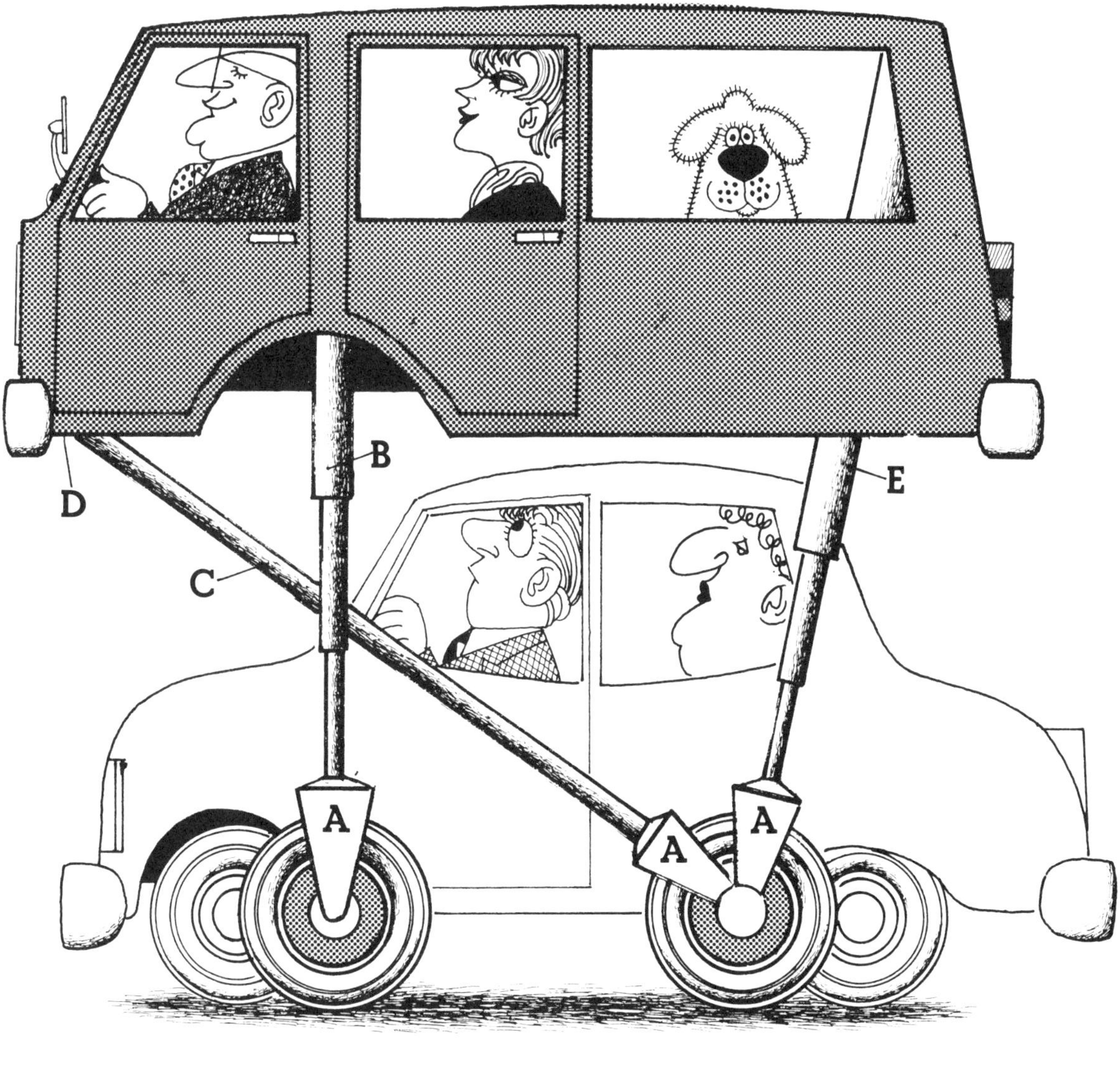
B
E
D
C
A
A
A

The Slimousine

How often has the top executive, chauffeur-driven in his luxury limousine, ground his teeth in anger as he sits motionless amid the idling engines of a traffic snarl in, say, Piccadilly Circus! On his way, perhaps, from Haymarket to an important directors' meeting in Portland Place, he has already spent two frustrating hours en route, each minute costing his company fortunes in lost time.

The Slimousine caters for this situation. In profile it is a superior, custom-built, top people's automobile, worthy of the grandest ambassador, potentate, foreign dignitary or royal personage. But, at less than a metre wide, it can thread its way through all but the most impossible traffic jams.

Under the Slimousine are two castor-ended stabilizers, normally carried in the position shown at X. However, should the vehicle exhibit any tendency to fall over, particularly when travelling at very low speed in a high wind, or if bumped into by a careless pedestrian, then, at the slightest sign of departure from the vertical the stabilisers automatically swing out sideways (Y), thus ensuring that the dignity of the important personage within encounters no risk of impairment.

Very large Slimousines, suitable for companies with numbers of top executives wishing to travel together, are jointed in several places, enabling them to weave through traffic as effortlessly as a snake making its way through thick jungle undergrowth. The different sections of these long but slender vehicles, still less than a metre wide, are supported on inconspicuous intermediate wheels (Z), giving great stability whilst detracting little from the required magnificent appearance.

Z

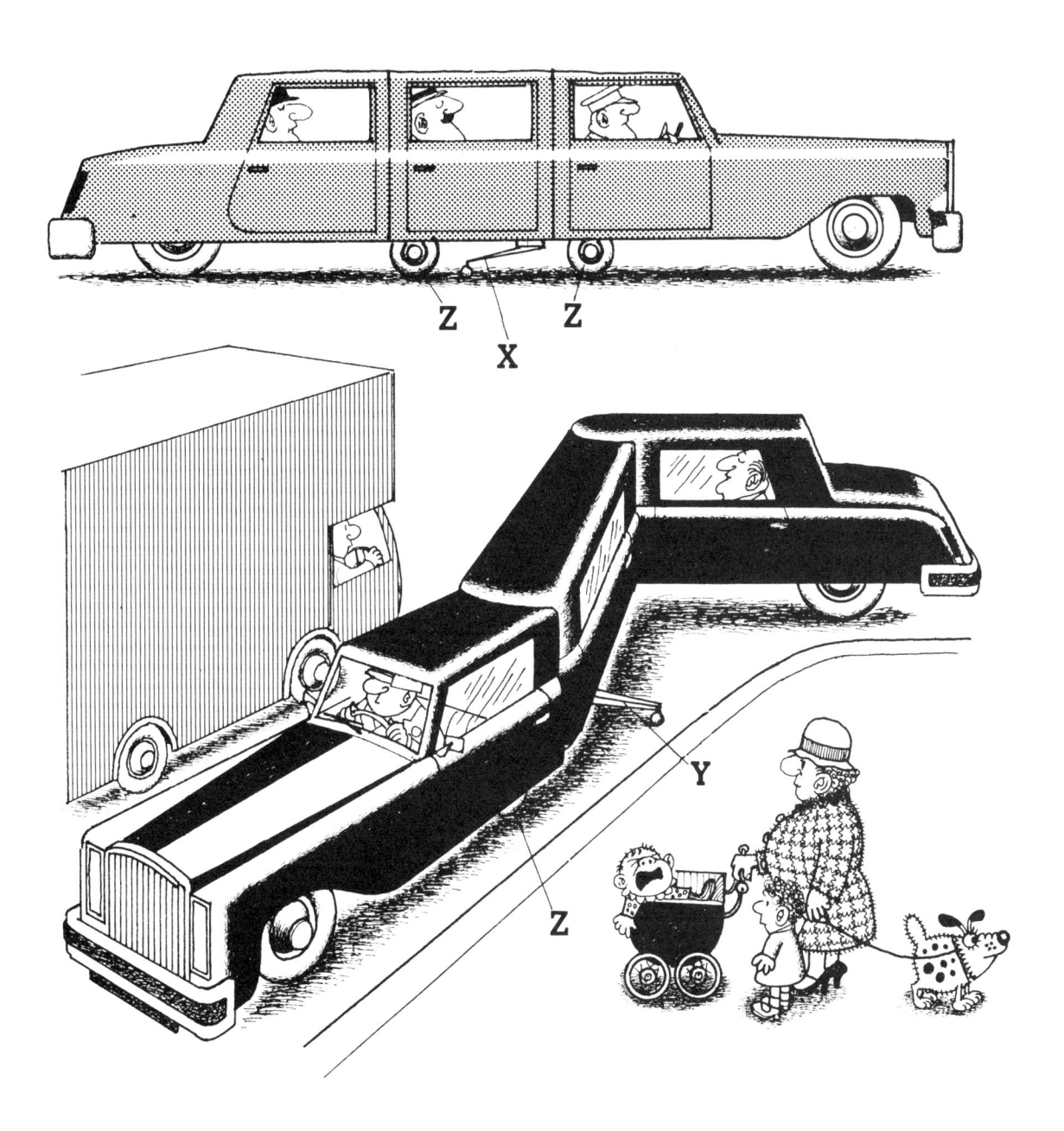

X

Z

Y

Z

The Swiveller

When you come to think of it, every automobile that has ever been built is an anachronism. Setting aside the archaic engine, identical in most essentials to that of the first of the horseless carriages, just look at the method of steering: two wheels at the front which can be steered to a limited extent and two at the back which can't! Yet we are required to pilot these obsolete contraptions through the densest traffic, to fit them into microscopic parking places, to turn them round in the narrowest of streets and generally perform the most daunting manœuvring feats.

Now that we are at the dusk of the motoring era, perhaps the Swiveller has come too late. But at least we can dream of what might have been. The Swiveller is mounted on a bogie (T) and balanced upon a sprung-pivot (U). The engine, arranged amidships in the bogie, drives all four wheels (V) (only two are visible in the illustration) through horizontal shafts to the four forks (W), each of which contains another vertical shaft for transmitting power to its wheel. All four forks are connected to the steering wheel (X) and hence are steerable, those at the back turning counter to the front ones. The Swiveller is thus extraordinarily manœuvrable and can turn almost in its own length. Controls are normal with the exception of a lever (Y) which when brought into operation rotates the entire car on its central pivot. One other extra control, the 'sidepark', turns all four wheels through 90 degrees.

Suppose you are driving the Swiveller along a road in a normal, unspectacular manner and wish to park in a space no longer than the car itself. Simple. After stopping the vehicle alongside the chosen spot you move the 'sidepark' control and the car drives sideways neatly into the space. Perhaps you wish to turn the car around in a busy street. Also simple—no manœuvring or three-point turns. By moving the lever (Y) you rotate the whole vehicle on its central pivot until it is facing the opposite direction, reverse the transmission, and then just drive off.

You may get bored with driving straight ahead in the ordinary way. You can turn the Swiveller sideways on its central pivot and proceed down the road broadside on. You can even 'waltz' the car from side to side or revolve it slowly while still continuing in a straight line. Bad for the fairground business but good fun for you.

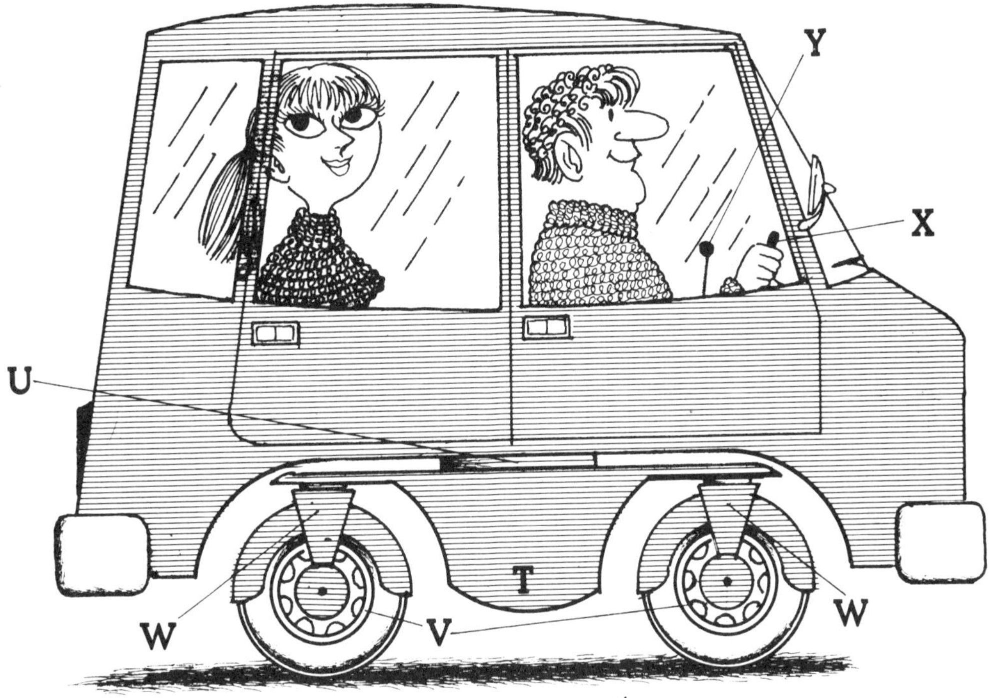
Y
X
U
T
W
V
W
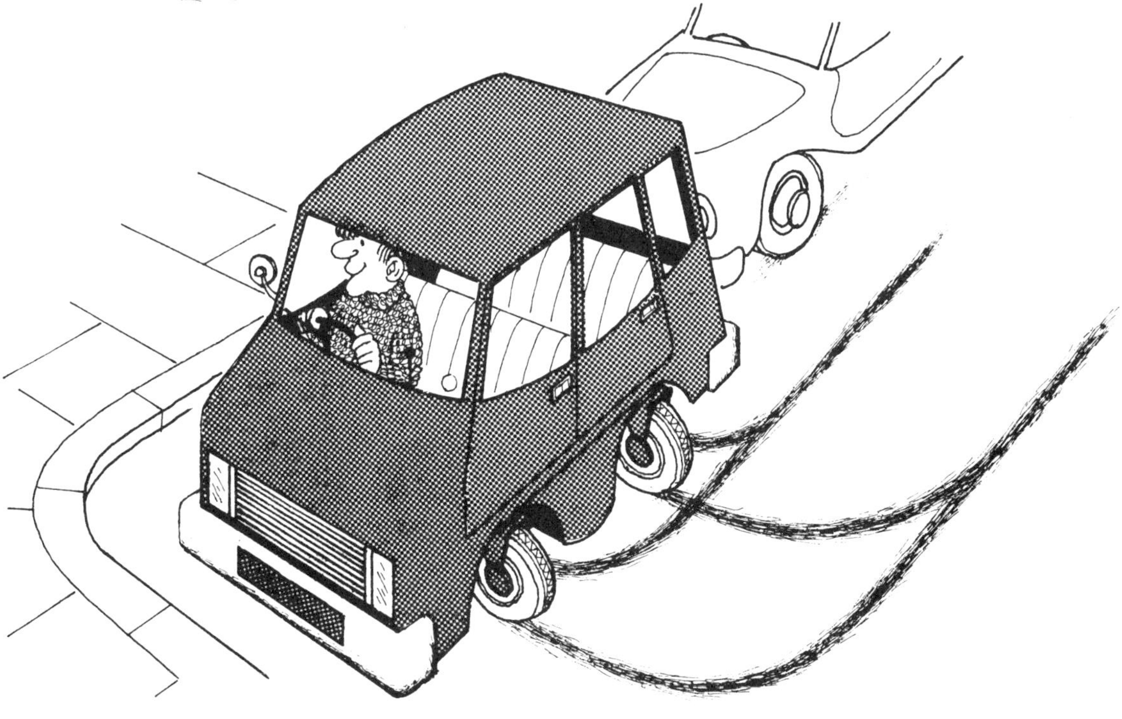

The Walking Stick

The pear-shaped profile of the average motorist persists as an unacceptable by-product of our modern motor age and we must face the unavoidable fact that the more solutions we find to the problems of mechanical transportation, the more departures we shall see from the original conception of the human form. Even if some of us manage to avoid the pear contour, few can escape that of the sausage. And it is all due to lack of exercise. Who knows? Pumpkin-shaped people may soon become quite common, incapable of walking from their automobiles to their front doors, and having to roll like footballs.

Exercise is the only answer—and for many generations 'walking the dog' has been a useful accessory towards this end. However the Walking Stick is now an alternative, more economical, and much less troublesome solution. It resembles a traditional walking stick in every way except for the ferrule end, which is equipped with small mechanical legs (A), driven by an electric motor (B) within the lower part of the stick shaft. The rest of the shaft is occupied by batteries and at the top, in the handle, is a timer (C) with speed control (D) and start button (E).

When the operator wants to go for a stroll he first decides how long he wants to walk for. Then he sets the timer, adjusts the speed control to his natural gait and presses the start button. The Stick immediately trots away, towing him behind it. An excellent discipline, as once the apparatus is started there is no way of stopping it until the preset amount of time has elapsed.

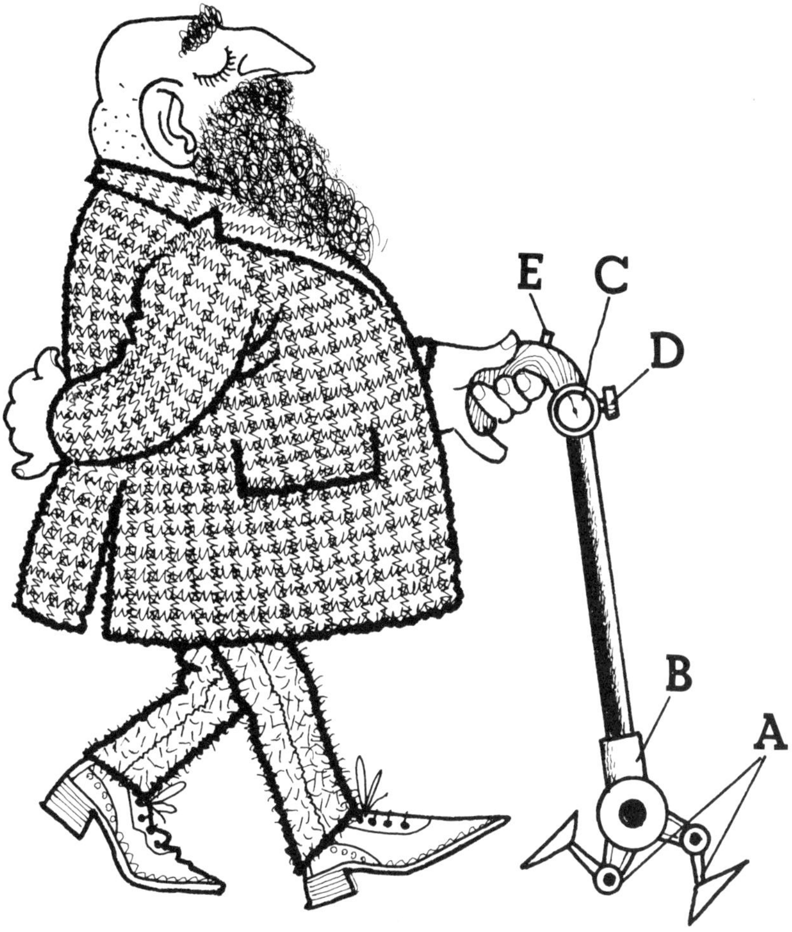
E
C
D
B
A